Second Seasoning Cookbook

Wes Miller

To
Helen,
Brian, Donna, Christopher,
Elijah, Dominic, Ezra,
Isabella, Henry, Nathan,
Spencer and Ashley.
God's gifts all.

Second Seasoning Cookbook – 2nd Edition

Photographs by Wes Miller
Illustrations in Appendix by Wes Miller

Front cover: Shrimp Hot Pot Soup
Back cover: Shrimp Lo Mein
Title page: Shrimp and Pork Egg Rolls

Table of Contents

Forward

I originally wanted to write a simple hand-me-down to my children with a few of the recipes that they fondly (so they say) remembered while growing up. The plan was to include about 10 to 20 of our family favorites. As I started to compile the recipes, I found I had to add just one more, and then just one more, and then "maybe they will like this one". So, then I decided to add ones that were my favorites, too. You can see the result.

My love of good food and cooking comes partly from my Italian ethnic upbringing on my mother's side of the family. Both of my grandparents on her side came to this country from "The Old Country" as children. As we all know, food, meals and family are a very important part of any Italian family. I remember big family holidays with all the relatives, as many as 40, all packed into someone's house. I remember all the food and all the preparation that started days ahead for homemade ravioli, baked stuffed shrimp, meatballs, sausage, linguini in white clam sauce, zappoles, struffoli, pies, and the list goes on. I tried to bring as much of this as possible to my children.

As I became older, my horizons broadened from the simple Italian and American food I had been brought up on and restricted myself to cooking. I discovered other ethnic cooking, especially Oriental cooking, and also, being brought up in New England, seafood played a big roll. Both of these areas are well represented in this book.

I also discovered (or always knew) that the only thing better than a good meal is a good sense of humor. My children grew up on good food and really good, or bad, puns or groaners. They all survived the torture (so far) that I put them through then, and still put them through to this day (ask any of them). They have all moved away and now have families of their own. But always when they visit, or I visit them, they have to put up with groaners to make the visit complete. Consequently, most of the recipes in this book have an accompanying groaner.

I thought it was only fair to cover all bases and pass these recipes down, along with the groaners, so that my children, grandchildren and anyone else who chooses, will be properly armed to suffer the same experiences that my children were brought up on (or subjected to). After all, a dry cookbook is just as bad as a dry steak, in my opinion. You will have to decide if this is a cookbook with groaners or a groaner book with recipes.

This is the third version of this book, correcting some obvious, and not so obvious mistakes, as well as adding new recipes seasoned with a dash of more humor. Hence: the title Second Seasoning Cookbook. Enjoy.

BREAKFAST

And so it begins … again …

Blueberry Muffins

"Start every day off with a smile and get it over with."
-W. C. Fields

Popovers

Popovers are the American version of Yorkshire pudding. The major difference is that American popovers are not cooked with meat drippings and are not usually spiced as with Yorkshire pudding.

This has to be a favorite of a lot of people. It's so easy to make. Make sure you have a good supply of jams, jellies and marmalades on hand. Usually served for breakfast or afternoon tea.

Ingredients:

- 1 cup **sifted** all-purpose flour
- ½ teaspoon salt
- 1 cup milk
- 2 eggs

Directions:

Preheat oven to 425° F. Place well-greased muffin tins or Pyrex type glass cups on the middle rack in the heated oven for about 5 minutes. Note that you should use the good old solid shortening (like Crisco) to heavily grease the tins and not the convenient sprays. The popovers will still stick if you use the spray. It is very important to <u>preheat the muffin tin or Pyrex</u>. The popovers will not "pop" unless you add the batter to a hot cup.

Place all the ingredients in a mixing bowl. Using an electric mixer beat all the ingredients just until smooth.

Open the oven door and slide out the rack with the cups or muffin tins. Fill each of the cups about 2/3 full of the batter. Do this as quickly as possible so that you do not lose a lot of heat from the oven. Cook until they are golden brown, about 35 to 45 minutes. Remove and serve immediately with butter or your choice of jelly or jam.

Makes about 8 popovers.

Popovers

A Hunter walking through the jungle found a huge dead elephant with a pigmy standing beside it.

Amazed, he asked: "Did you kill that?"

The pigmy said, "Yes."

The hunter asked, "How could a little bloke like you kill a huge beast like that?"

"I killed it with my club."

The astonished hunter asked, "How big is your club?"

The pigmy replied, "There's about 60 of us."

Mom's Blueberry Muffins

Mom perfected this recipe and passed it down. This is one of the few recipes that I measure the ingredients very carefully, although Mom was known to use more than 2 cups of fresh blueberries. This makes awesome muffins every time.

Ingredients:

- ½ cup butter (1 stick), softened
- 1 cup sugar
- 2 eggs, beaten
- ¾ cup whole milk
- ½ teaspoon vanilla
- 2 cups flour
- 2 teaspoons baking powder
- ½ teaspoon salt
- 1 teaspoon ground cinnamon
- ¼ teaspoon ground nutmeg
- 2 cups fresh blueberries, (may use frozen, but they are never as good as fresh)
- 2 tablespoons sugar or however much desired, for topping

Preparations:

In a medium-mixing bowl, cream together the butter and sugar until smooth. Add the eggs and mix well. Stir in the milk and vanilla. Combine all the dry ingredients and add to the mixture and mix well. Add the blueberries and <u>gently</u> fold them into the batter. Fill well greased muffin cups about ¾ full. Sprinkle sugar over the tops of each muffin to taste. Bake in a preheated 375° F oven for 20 minutes, or until lightly browned.

Serve hot or cold.

Makes about a dozen muffins.

Blueberry Muffins

Two silk worms had a race. They ended up in a tie.

Pancakes

This is probably one of the first things I learned to cook on my own. That is probably because pancakes date back to prehistoric times. How they know this, I am not quite sure. I have never heard of fossilized pancakes being discovered anywhere. But they go back to MY prehistoric times I know. My kids grew up with this recipe, too. They seemed to think there was something special about them, until they learned to make them themselves; then I lost all credit. Everyone loves these pancakes. Use the same recipe for waffles.

Ingredients:

- 1 egg
- 1¼ cups of sour milk
- ½ teaspoon baking soda
- 1¼ cups all purpose flour
- 1 teaspoon sugar
- 2 tablespoons vegetable oil
- 1 teaspoon baking powder
- ½ teaspoon salt

Directions:

Make the sour milk by taking 1 cup of milk and ¼ cup white vinegar, let curdle. Mix all the ingredients thoroughly, adding wet to dry, and let sit for a few minutes until you see the bubbles rising.

Heat griddle until hot (a drop of water will skittle across the surface when dropped). Add a tablespoon of oil and spread it around. Using a ladle pour each of the pancakes on the griddle. Cook until air bubbles start to form uniformly across the pancake and then flip them.

Serve immediately with maple syrup and any fruit topping you wish, such as banana slices, strawberries, or blueberries.

For good old Blueberry Pancakes, fold in, not stir, the blueberries carefully after the other ingredients have been mixed making sure not to break open the berries or you will get blue pancakes.

I usually make a double batch … they go fast.

I used to work at an orange juice factory,
but I was canned because I couldn't concentrate.

French Toast

French toast is one of the easiest recipes you will find anywhere,
fluffy and tender on the inside and gloriously browned on the outside.
This is always a favorite with the kids.

Ingredients:

- 4 eggs
- 2/3 cup whole milk
- 2 teaspoons cinnamon (optional)
- 8 slices of 2-day-old bread (better if slightly stale)
- Butter
- Maple syrup

Directions:

Preheat a large skillet over medium high heat.

In a medium sized bowl, whisk the eggs, milk and cinnamon (if using). Whisk until well blended and pour into a shallow bowl wide enough to place a piece of bread that you are using. I find a pie plate works well. Melt some butter in the skillet.

Place each slice of bread into the egg mixture and coat each side well allowing the mixture to absorb some into the bread. Shake off any excess egg mixture from the bread and place as many pieces will fit on the hot skillet. Fry until brown on one side and then turn over to the other side, when done plate it and serve hot with butter, maple syrup and any other topping desired, like fresh fruit.

A missionary in the deepest Amazon suddenly finds himself surrounded by a bloodthirsty group of natives. Upon surveying his situation, he says quietly to himself, "I'm toast."

A ray of light breaks forth from the sky and a voice booms out: "No, you are NOT toast. Pick up that stone in front of you and bash the head of the chief."

So the missionary picks up the stone and proceeds to bash the head of the chief, knocking him out. He is breathing heavily while standing above the sprawled out-chief.

Surrounding him are the 100 native warriors with a look of shock on their faces. The voice booms out again: "Okay...NOW you're toast!"

Biscuits and Sausage Gravy

This is an Old West favorite that was served on the cattle drives. Cattle drives are kind of like morning commutes to work. Easy to make and good breakfast alternative. I picked up this recipe while living in Colorado.

Ingredients:

- 2 pounds bulk breakfast sausage (such as Jimmie Dean's)
- 2-4 tablespoons butter
- 4 tablespoons all purpose flour
- 4 cups cold milk
- Salt and pepper to taste
- 12 Biscuits - Refrigerated packaged biscuits of your choice or make from scratch

Directions:

Make the biscuits. While they are cooking heat a stainless or cast iron pan over high heat. Do not use non-stick pans since you want to get all those brown bits that will stick to the bottom of the pan. Crumble the sausage up as much as possible and cook.

Once the sausage is browned all over, remove it to a bowl using a slotted spoon. Leave the rendered fat and brown bits in the pan; they are needed to make the roux.

Lower the heat to low. You should use one tablespoon of flour for each tablespoon of fat. Add additional butter to the rendered fat to make up the difference. When the butter is nearly melted, add the flour and stir. Keep stirring until the flour is completely incorporated, and the roux starts to turn the barest shade darker. Add the milk, turn the heat up to medium, and scrape up as much as you can of the bits stuck to the bottom of the pan. Add salt and pepper to taste. The gravy should be fairly thick.

Add the sausage back in and stir until the sausage is warmed back up. Transfer the sausage gravy to a serving bowl and cover it with a plate to keep the heat and steam in.

Split the still warm biscuits in half horizontally and cover them with warm sausage gravy and serve.

Serves about 4

I wondered why the baseball was getting bigger. Then it hit me.

LUNCH

Thick Crust Mushroom Pizza

"Ask not what you can do for your country, ask what's for lunch."
– Orson Wells

Italian Sausage Calzone

The word Calzone comes from the Italian word meaning "stocking" or "trouser leg"; at least that's what I read. This dish is a bit of a task to do, but so worth it, especially if you have a crowd to please. Guido's favorite lunch! **This makes two very large Calzones**.

Ingredients:

- Pizza dough (enough for 1 large or 2 medium pizzas), see recipe
- 1 pound mild or sweet Italian sausages
- ½ large green pepper, diced
- 1 medium sized onion, diced
- 4 ounces of mushrooms
- Mozzarella cheese (shredded)
- Parmesan Cheese (shredded)
- 1 8-ounce can of tomato sauce
- 1 tablespoon olive oil
- Handful of fresh cilantro
- Small handful of fresh Italian parsley
- 1 egg
- 1 tablespoon of water
- 1 tablespoon milk
- Salt and pepper

Directions:

Prepare the sausage by removing the sausage meat from its casing and breaking it up into very small pieces; by hand is the best way. Chop the mushrooms into ½ inch by ¼ inch pieces. Beat the egg with the water in a small bowl and set aside.

Put the oil in a large skillet and heat over medium high heat until the oil is just about to smoke. Add the sausage and stir-fry until just about done, about 3 to 4 minutes. Add the mushrooms, onion and pepper and cook for another minute. Lower the heat to medium and add the tomato sauce. Mix while cooking, adding salt and pepper to taste, for about 2 minutes. Remove from heat and set aside until cool (room temperature).

Preheat the oven to 425° F. Cut the pizza dough into two equal pieces. Take one piece of the dough and roll it out into a circle about 12 to 15 inches across. Let it sit for a minute to let it shrink a bit.

Add ½ of the cooled sausage mixture on one half of the rolled out dough leaving the other half empty. Make sure you leave about 1 inch of dough on the edge free of the filling for binding the crust. Top the filling with the cheeses to taste.

Brush the inside of the crust edge with milk then take the upper half of the dough and cover the filling and match up the edges to form a half-circle. Pinch the edges like a piecrust to seal the dough and so no filling will leak out. Slice three 2-inch slits in the top of the Calzone to allow steam to escape so the filling will not force out the sides. Repeat for the other half of the dough.

Calzone Filling

Place Calzones on a piece of parchment paper and, with a pastry brush, coat the entire dough with the egg wash. Place in the oven and cook for 15 to 20 minutes or until the dough is golden brown. Remove from the oven and let cool for a few minutes before serving. Serves 4.

Italian Sausage Calzone

Dogs can't operate MRI scanners, but catscan.

Making A Better BLT

This isn't so much about the ingredients; after all, a bacon, lettuce, and tomato (BLT) sandwich is nothing too special. You use your favorite bacon, use your preferred kind of lettuce and tomato and place it between your favorite bread, toasted or not, with some kind of mayonnaise. But, here is something I bet you never thought of.

If you are like most people, you like your BLT on toasted bread, but toast has its pluses and minuses. On the plus side, the toast prevents the bread from absorbing the mayo and juices in the sandwich, therefore preventing it from getting soggy, and it keeps the sandwich firm and prevents the contents from slipping out when you bite into it. On the negative side, eating a dry toast sandwich scratches the roof of your mouth, which isn't very pleasant or at the very least annoying.

The solution: Toast just one side of each piece of bread putting the toasted side on the inside of the sandwich! By toasting just the inside of the bread you can reap all the benefits of toast and eliminate that nasty roof of the mouth problem. The sandwich stays firm, doesn't get soggy and also has a rather special "something" that makes you think, "Now why didn't I think of this before?" An easy way to do this is to put two slices of bread together in the toaster. The outside of each will toast and the inside will stay un-toasted.

You might want to try this on any sandwich that you might like toasted; chicken, turkey, tuna, you name it.

There once was a king who lived in a two-story grass hut. Every holiday the king demanded to be given a new throne as a gift. As soon as a new throne arrived, he would store the old throne on the second level of his hut and use the new one instead. But one day the hut collapsed from the weight of all the thrones, and everyone was crushed and killed.

The moral of this story? Those who live in grass houses shouldn't stow thrones.

Shrimp Po' Boy

A little New Orleans fare here with just enough "kick" to make you want more. You can also use oysters instead of shrimp. This recipe makes two very large, generous Po' Boys, but could easily serve 4. When I cook, I cook big!

Ingredients:

- 12 to16 21/24 count or 10 to12 16/20 count shrimp, peeled and deveined
- ½ cup Flour
- ½ teaspoon Cayenne (or to taste)
- 1 teaspoon Kosher Salt
- 1 teaspoon Onion powder
- 1 teaspoon Paprika
- ½ teaspoon freshly ground pepper
- 1 egg
- 2 tablespoons Milk
- Peanut or vegetable oil for deep frying
- Fresh French baguette bread
- Lettuce
- Tomato, sliced

Sauce
- 4 Tablespoon Mayonnaise
- ½teaspoon Paprika
- ¼ teaspoon Cayenne (or to taste)
- ½ teaspoon Onion powder
- ½ teaspoon Garlic powder
- 2 teaspoon Lemon juice

Directions:

Make the sauce by combining all the ingredients and mixing well. Set aside.

Mix the milk with the egg; add the shrimp and let stand for 3 minutes.

Split the baguettes and remove most of the soft white bread from the center of each half allowing room for the shrimp and "fixin's".

Mix the flour, cayenne, salt, onion powder, paprika and pepper. Dredge the shrimp coating them well with mixture. Cook the shrimp in batches in hot oil at 375° F. until golden brown. Remove and place on a rack to drain while the other shrimp are cooking.

Generously coat each side of the baguette with the sauce, and then add the lettuce, tomato and shrimp. Serve while shrimp is still hot.

Shrimp Po' Boy

A sandwich walks into a bar. The bartender says, "Sorry we don't serve food here."

Fajitas – Chicken, Steak or Shrimp

Whether or not you are a great lover of Mexican food, you have to love fajitas. Make these fajitas with whichever filling you want to use … chicken, steak or shrimp. Fajitas are usually served on a sizzling platter in restaurants with tortillas on the side.

Ingredients:

- 3 boneless skinless chicken breasts or 1 pound of flank, flat iron (the most flavorful) or skirt steak or 1 to 1 ½ lbs large shrimp (shelled and deveined)
- 1 green bell pepper
- 1 red pepper
- 1 yellow pepper
- 1 large Portobello mushroom cap
- 1 large white or yellow onion
- 2 tablespoons olive oil
- Parsley for garnish
- 8 large tortillas
- Tomato salsa (see My Tomato Salsa recipe)
- Sour cream

Marinade:

- 2 limes
- ½ pack of fresh Cilantro (1/3 cup chopped)
- 2 tablespoons of dried Oregano
- ½ teaspoon of Chili pepper
- ½ teaspoon sugar
- 1 teaspoon Cumin (or to taste)
- 1 tablespoon olive oil
- Salt and fresh ground pepper
- Optional: 2 cloves garlic (minced), 1 jalapeno pepper seeded and chopped (only if you like it really spicy)

If using meat, slice into thin long strips cutting against the grain for tenderness.

Grate the rind of one of the limes into a bowl then squeeze the juice from both. Into this, add the rest of the marinade ingredients and season with salt and pepper. Mix together well.

Add the meat strips or shrimp and mix until all the pieces are coated. Set aside to marinate for at least 30 minutes – however, the longer you can leave it, the more the juices will soak in. I prefer to place it all in a zip lock back and refrigerate for about 3 or four hours, turning the bag a few times to mix.

Cut each of the peppers and mushrooms into long thin strips. Thinly slice the onion with the grain so that there will be long thin pieces. Keep each of the vegetables, and each pepper type, separate since they will be cooked at different times.

Heat the oil in the large skillet or griddle over a high heat until smoking hot. Add the meat or shrimp and all the marinade and stir-fry until tender, approximately 4-5 minutes or, for the shrimp, when they are all pink (do not overcook the shrimp). Plate the meat or shrimp. Add more oil and heat the pan again until smoking. Add the green peppers and onions and cook for about 2 minutes stirring constantly. Add the red and yellow peppers and mushrooms. Continue cooking for 2 more minutes until the vegetables are just start to get soft. Salt and pepper as needed.

Return the meat or shrimp to the vegetables and stir for about a minute mixing completely. Plate or keep in the hot skillet, garnish with chopped parsley, lime slices and serve.

Put the mixture into a warmed flour tortilla, then add sour cream and tomato salsa then roll it up and enjoy.

Serving 4 people, 2 fajitas each.

A man goes into a bar and orders a beer. He takes a sip of the beer and a small voice say's "Nice Tie!!"

The man looks around and doesn't see anyone. A little puzzled he takes another sip, and again the voice says "Nice shirt Too!!!"

Now the man calls the bartender back and complains that every time he takes a sip of beer he hears a small voice.

The bartender says "Oh never mind that! That's just the peanuts, they're complimentary!!

Chicken Nuggets

I bet that chicken nuggets are more popular at fast food restaurants than burgers. Kids love them. So why not make them at home? After an exhaustive search of different nuggets (that used real chicken, that is), I've decided that this is the best recipe you'll find anywhere.

Ingredients:

- 1 pound boneless, skinless chicken breasts, cut into bite sized pieces
- 1 ½ cups milk
- ½ cup dill pickle juice
- 1 egg
- ¼ cup all-purpose flour
- ½ cup cornstarch
- ½ cup corn flour (not corn meal)
- ½ cup confectioner's sugar
- 2 teaspoons baking powder
- Salt and freshly ground black pepper
- Peanut oil for frying

Directions:

In a large bowl, combine chicken, ½ cup milk and pickle juice. Cover and place in the refrigerator for at least 2 hours or overnight; drain well.

Heat the peanut oil in a large skillet over medium high heat, or you can use a deep fryer set to 375° F.

In a large bowl, whisk together remaining 1 cup of milk and egg. Stir in chicken and gently toss to combine; drain excess milk mixture.

In a gallon size Ziploc bag or large bowl, combine the chicken, flour, baking powder and confectioners' sugar. Season with salt and pepper, to taste.

Working in batches, add chicken to the skillet or deep fryer and cook until evenly golden and crispy, about 2-3 minutes. Transfer to a paper towel-lined plate.

You can keep them warm in a 250° F oven. Serve with dipping sauce of your choice.

He who dies with the most toys is nonetheless dead.

Seafood Pasta Salad

At a party many years ago I was introduced to cold Calamari Salad. I've loved it ever since and have expanded it to a Seafood Salad.

Ingredients:

- 1 pound box of large Rotini or Rotelle pasta
- 1 pound squid/calamari rings
- 1 pound shrimp 21/25 count, peeled and deveined
- 1 8 ounce package of imitation crabmeat
- 4+ tablespoons olive oil
- 1 tablespoon minced garlic
- 2 tablespoons of salt
- Onion salt
- Garlic salt
- Fresh ground pepper
- Finely chopped parsley
- Optional: Finely chopped basil, finely chopped scallions

Directions:

Fill a large saucepan 2/3 full of water and bring to a boil. Add the tablespoon of salt to the water and then add the Rotini. Cook until al dente, drain and rinse with cold water to stop the cooking and set aside. While the pasta is cooking, cut up the crabmeat into bite-sized pieces and place in a large 1-gallon or larger sized bowl. Add about 1 tablespoon of olive oil, mix and season with the garlic salt, onion salt and pepper to taste, but not too strong because more will be added later.

Fill the same saucepan used with the pasta half full of water and bring to a boil. Add 1 tablespoon of salt and then add the calamari. Cook for 2 to 3 minutes, remove, drain and rinse with cold water to stop the cooking process. Separately, do the same with the shrimp, or better, poach the shrimp as in the poached shrimp recipe.

When everything has cooled down to just about room temperature, add the garlic, calamari, shrimp, pasta, and about 3 tablespoons of olive oil to the crabmeat. Mix until all is coated with the oil. Season with onion salt, garlic salt, pepper, parsley and optional seasonings to taste. Cover the bowl and refrigerate for at least an hour. Serve cold

Serves 6 as a main course. Tightly cover and refrigerate. It will keep for several days. You may want to add more oil the next day since the pasta tends to absorb any liquid. Makes for great lunch or appetizer. Great to just pick on right out of the fridge.

Seafood Pasta Salad

A snake slithers into a bar and the bartender says, "Sorry, buddy. I can't serve you."

"Why not?" the snake asks.

"Because you can't hold your liquor."

Super-Simple Rib Eye Beef Sandwich

There are so many Rib Eye steak sandwich recipes out there, I've come to believe that each one is just trying to outdo the other, or be more fanciful, or whatever. Although sometimes delicious, I find that when you add too many condiments or spices, you lose the flavor of the steak. So, try not to overpower the sandwich with too many spices. Thin sliced Rib Eyes are usually available at most grocers, if not, they will gladly slice them for you at the butcher counter.

Ingredients:

- ½ lb. thin sliced Rib Eye steak per sandwich
- 1 8-inch fresh submarine sandwich roll per sandwich
- 2 tablespoons of butter per sandwich
- Salt
- Pepper

Optional fixin's:

- Lettuce
- Sliced tomato
- Mayonnaise
- Barbeque sauce
- Sliced cheese (American, Provolone, or your choice)
- Sautéed onions
- Sautéed mushrooms

Directions:

If you are going to use sautéed onions or mushrooms, cook them first and then set aside.

Salt and pepper both sides of each of the Rib Eyes.

Split the rolls down the middle lengthwise and liberally butter both insides.

Heat a large skillet over medium high heat and toast the buttered side of the rolls until golden brown. Remove the rolls and put on a serving plate.

In the same skillet, melt the remaining butter and make sure it covers the whole skillet. Pan fry the steaks about 1 minute per side or until the desired doneness is achieved. If using cheese, you may desire to top the steaks with the cheese while cooking to second side so it will melt.

Put steaks on the toasted rolls, add desired options and condiments and enjoy!

Turning vegan would be a big missed steak.

Pizza Dough

There are three ways to prepare pizza dough; the basic manual method, the bread machine method, or buying pre-made dough at the grocery store. The first two are covered below. I would hope you don't need instruction for the third method. Pizza dough is used in several different recipes in this book besides pizza.

Basic dough, the manual way:

- 1 packages rapid rise dry yeast
- 1¼ cups warm beer*
- 4 tablespoons olive oil or butter (melted)
- ¼ teaspoon salt
- 2 teaspoon sugar
- 2¾ cups flour
- ½ cup cornmeal

Sprinkle yeast and sugar into warm beer in small bowl; allow stand, about 5 minutes. It's supposed to be foamy.

Mix flour, cornmeal, oil (or butter) and salt in a large bowl; make a well in the center and add yeast mixture. Stir to form a soft dough, adding more flour if necessary. Remove the dough and place on a floured board and knead until dough is supple and elastic, about 7 to 10 minutes of muscle work.

Transfer to a large bowl. Cover the bowl with plastic wrap to seal from outside air and let dough rise in a warm spot until dough has doubled in size, about 1 hour. Punch down dough. Put back in the bowl, cover and let rise again; then punch down a second time.

Transfer to a lightly floured surface; roll dough to a 13-inch circle. Transfer to an oiled 12–inch deep-dish pizza pan; spread the dough to evenly cover the pan with the dough coming up the sides of the pan to form a dish. You must also decide if you want a thick or thin crust pizza.

* Choose the beer very carefully. A weak or light beer will not be as flavorful as a full-bodied beer.

Basic dough, the easy way, using a bread machine:

Use the basic pizza dough recipe that came with the bread maker replacing water with beer and optionally add 2 tablespoons of soft or melted butter. Try to keep the ingredients as close to the ones given above. Process using the dough setting of the bread machine; this typically takes about 2 hours, but saves a lot of work!

Hawaiian Pizza (Ham and Pineapple).

You just don't get them this good from a pizza store!

Did you hear about the guy whose whole left side was cut off? He's all right now.

Shrimp Scampi Pizza

This is a simply awesome pizza and is sure to impress guests. Just don't put too much of the liquid mixture on the pizza or you will have a run-off problem when you move the pizza out of the oven and when you cut it.

Ingredients:

- 13-16 ounces pizza dough
- 8 ounces sliced or shredded mozzarella
- 1 tablespoon olive oil
- 2 pounds medium to large shrimp, peeled and deveined (26/30 count works well)
- 2 tablespoons finely chopped garlic
- ½ cup white wine
- ¼ cup chicken stock
- 2 tablespoons lemon juice
- Kosher salt and freshly ground black pepper
- 4 tablespoons butter
- 2 tablespoons fresh parsley leaves, chopped

Directions:

Preheat oven to 450° F.

Stretch pizza dough to make a 16-inch pizza. Top crust with mozzarella, and bake on a pizza pan or pizza stone for 5 minutes or until the crust just starts to brown. Crust will only be partially cooked.

In a medium skillet over high heat, heat the olive oil until very hot and starts to shimmer. Remove the skillet from heat, add the shrimp and garlic, and toss. Lower the heat to simmer, put the pan back and add wine, chicken stock and lemon juice and bring to a simmer. Add the butter in 1-tablespoon pats, and heat until melted, and then remove from heat. Season mixture with salt and pepper to taste. Shrimp will finish cooking on the pizza.

Spread mixture over the partially cooked crust and finish baking until golden brown, about 5 minutes. There may be a lot of liquid if the shrimp retained water, so put just enough of the mixture over the pizza to cover the cheese. Sprinkle with chopped parsley. Let cool a few minutes before cutting.

Shrimp Scampi Pizza

Two boll weevils grew up in South Carolina. One went to Hollywood and became a famous actor. The other stayed behind in the cotton fields and never amounted to much. The second one, naturally, became known as the lesser of two weevils.

Chicago Deep-Dish Pizza

Pizza … what can I say about pizza that you don't already know? Chicago Deep-Dish Pizza is just a variation to get away from the same old, same old. The big deal is that the cheese goes on first, the sauce goes on top, and it is very thick.

Ingredients:

- ½ pound sliced mozzarella cheese
- Pizza dough (see recipe)
- 2 cups Italian-style crushed tomatoes
- 1 teaspoon basil
- 1 teaspoon oregano
- 3 cloves garlic, minced
- 3 tablespoons grated Parmesan cheese
- 3 tablespoons olive oil
- Salt and pepper to taste

Directions:

Oil a deep-dish pizza pan (make sure you use a deep-dish pan) or use a non-stick vegetable spray to coat. Place the dough in the pan and push it out to the edges using your fingers. Put in enough dough so that you can run the crust right up the side of the pan, about 1/8-inch thick throughout the pan as a minimum.

Place the cheese in tile-like layers on the bottom of the pie covering all the dough. Next put in the tomatoes and then the basil, oregano, garlic, and salt, reserving the Parmesan cheese for the top. Drizzle olive oil over the top of the pie and you are ready to bake.

Bake the pie in a 475° F oven until the top is golden and gooey and the crust a light golden brown, about 25 to 30 minutes. Let cool for about 5 minutes before cutting.

Variations: Before you put on the Parmesan cheese and olive oil drizzle or, if you desire, even before you add the tomatoes, add any or all of the following:

- Italian sausage, sliced or crumbled, hot or mild
- Yellow onions, peeled and chopped
- Pepperoni, thinly sliced
- Mushrooms, sliced
- Green sweet bell peppers, cored and sliced thin
- Ground beef
- Ham with optional pineapple
- Canadian bacon
- Shrimp, scallops, lobster or anything else you can come up with

Chicago Deep-Dish Pizza

What do you call cheese that isn't yours?   Nacho Cheese.

APPETIZERS

Crispy Fried Shrimp, Chinese Style

"Food is an important part of a balanced diet." – Fran Lebowitz

Crispy Fried Chicken Wings

A nice light batter on these wings makes them extra desirable with
just the right level of crispness.

Ingredients:

- About 10-12 full chicken wings
- 1 egg, beaten
- 1 tablespoon cornstarch
- 2 teaspoons sherry
- ¼ teaspoon salt
- Oil for frying

Batter:

- ½ cup all-purpose flour
- ½ cup chicken stock or water
- 3 tablespoons cornstarch
- 1 tablespoon vegetable oil
- ½ teaspoon baking soda
- ½ teaspoon salt

Directions:

Cut the wings at the joints making drummettes and wingettes. Save the wing tips for making stock if desired. Mix the egg, 1 tablespoon of cornstarch, the wine and ¼ teaspoon of salt in a bowl. Stir in the wings to coat and place in the refrigerator for 10 minutes.

Heat the oil in a large saucepan, wok or deep fryer to 375° F. In a bowl, mix the flour, chicken stock, cornstarch, 1 tablespoon of oil, the baking soda and salt. Add the chicken and stir until coated. Fry no more than 6 pieces at a time, turning occasionally, until golden brown, about 3 minutes. Drain. Serve hot with the dipping sauce of your choice if desired.

Crispy Fried Wings

A chicken crossing the road: poultry in motion.

Honey Bourbon Chicken Wings

I wonder. Do I have more shrimp recipes or chicken wing recipes?
Now these are broiled rather than baked.

Ingredients:

- One dozen wings into drumettes and wingettes, tips discarded (save for stock)
- Onion salt, garlic salt and pepper to taste

Marinade:

- ½ cup honey
- ½ cup Bourbon
- 1 tablespoon lemon juice
- 1 teaspoon garlic powder
- 1 teaspoon onion powder
- 1 teaspoon freshly ground pepper

Directions:

Place all the marinade ingredients into a bowl and mix until homogeneous. Put marinade and chicken into plastic bag, seal it and refrigerate for at least 4 hours, or even better overnight, mixing the contents several times.

Remove the bag from the refrigerator and let stand until almost room temperature.

Spray a cooking rack with non-stick spray and place the chicken on the rack evenly spaced. Sprinkle with onion salt, garlic salt and fresh ground pepper to taste. Broil each side until golden brown and done. Serve immediately.

When you are down by the sea
And an eel bites your knee
That's a moray

Hoisin-Ginger Chicken Wings

This is a baked Oriental style appetizer instead of the usual fried or broiled. I always like the ones you can prepare ahead of time. This one cooks up with a nice flavored sauce coating.

Ingredients:

- One dozen wings cut into drumettes and wingettes, tips discarded (save for stock). Total of two-dozen pieces.

Marinade

- 1/3 cup soy sauce
- ¼ cup Hoisin sauce
- ¼ cup rice vinegar
- 3 tablespoons brown sugar
- 4 garlic cloves, minced
- 1 tablespoon vegetable oil
- 2 teaspoons minced ginger
- 2 teaspoon sesame oil
- ¼ teaspoon red pepper flakes

Directions:

Mix the marinade ingredients well and place in a plastic zip lock bag with the chicken pieces. Marinade in the refrigerator for at least 4 hours up to 24 hours turning the bag every so often for even marinating.

Remove wings and place on wire rack or foil covered baking sheet. Bake in a 350° F oven for 30 minutes. The wings will look just "wet" when placed on the rack, but, a nice sauce will form during baking. Serve hot.

I childproofed my home, but they still get in.

Cranberried Chicken Wings

Almost like a mini-Thanksgiving. This is yet another recipe that can be
made ahead of time and is baked, not fried.

Ingredients:

- Two dozen wings into drumettes and wingettes, tips discarded (save for stock)
- 1 16-ounce can of jellied cranberry sauce
- 2 teaspoons brown sugar
- 1 ½ teaspoons prepared mustard
- 1 ½ teaspoons Worcestershire Sauce

Directions:

In a medium saucepan, combine the cranberry sauce, brown sugar, Worcestershire Sauce and mustard. Heat over low heat, stirring constantly, until the sauce is smooth. Remove from the heat and let cool.

Put the chicken pieces in a plastic zip lock bag and add the sauce. Marinade in the refrigerator for at least 4 hours or overnight.

Bake in a 350° F oven for 30 minutes.

Two antennas meet on a roof, fall in love and get married.
The ceremony wasn't much, but the reception was excellent.

Teriyaki Chicken Wings

So, who doesn't like teriyaki chicken? The recipe for homemade teriyaki sauce is in the sauces section. Look for the other teriyaki recipes; Baked Teriyaki Chicken and Teriyaki Tuna Steak, in this book.

Ingredients:

- One dozen wings cut into drumettes and wingettes, tips discarded (save for stock)
- ½ cup teriyaki sauce (see recipe in sauces or choose one from other recipe in book)
- ¾ chopped green onions
- 3 cloves chopped garlic
- Pepper

Directions:

Cut the wings at the joints into three pieces and save the wingtips for making stock. Combine all ingredients and pour over wings placed in a 10 x 6 x 1½ inch baking pan. Cover with foil and marinate ½ hour. Bake covered for 30 minutes at 350° F. Remove foil and turn wings once. Let brown until almost all liquid has absorbed.

The golfer sliced a ball into a field of chickens, striking one of the hens and killing it instantly. He was understandably upset, and sought out the farmer.

"I'm sorry," he said, "my terrible tee-shot hit one of your hens and killed it. Can I replace the hen?"

"I don't know about that," replied the farmer, mulling it over. "How many eggs a day do you lay?"

Sesame-Curry Chicken Wings

For all you curry fans out there. And yet another baked wing recipe.
I'm not a big curry fan, but these I like.

Ingredients:

- One dozen wings into drumettes and wingettes, tips discarded (save for stock)
- 1¼ cups Panko breadcrumbs
- 2 eggs
- 1 tablespoon soy sauce
- 1 teaspoon onion salt
- ½ teaspoon pepper
- 2 tablespoons curry powder
- ¼ cup sesame seeds
- ½ cup flour
- 1/3 cup butter, melted

Directions:

Beat the eggs with the soy sauce. Combine the breadcrumbs, onion salt, curry powder, pepper and sesame seeds in a separate bowl. Have the flour ready in another bowl or dish.

One at a time, dredge each wing piece in the flour, shaking off the excess. Next dip the wing in the eggs mixture to completely coat. Roll the wing in the breadcrumb mixture to make sure each piece is completely covered with the mixture. Place on a wire rack for baking.

Once all the wings are on the rack, drizzle them all with the melted butter. Bake in a 350° F oven for 30 minutes.

Serve hot.

Crushing pop cans is soda pressing.

Marinating Wings
Cranberried Wings, Hoisin-Ginger Wings and Sesame-Curry Wings

Wings!
Clockwise from top right:
Sesame-Curry Wings, Hoisin-Ginger Wings, Teriyaki Wings, and Cranberried Wings

Italian Sausage Appetizer in Wonton Cups

This fancy looking recipe is absolutely delicious and great for entertaining large groups. You can make these to your own taste by using different kinds of sausage, different cheeses and even using ranch dressing. These are always a hit.

Ingredients:

- 1 package Johnsonville Italian Sausage
- 2 cups shredded cheddar cheese
- 1 small red bell pepper, finely chopped
- ½ cup mayonnaise
- 24 wontons cups (see below)
- Olive oil for wontons
- Parsley for garnish

Directions:

To make the wonton cups:

Preheat the oven to 350°.

With a pastry brush, lightly brush each wonton (do one at a time) on both sides. Put each wonton in muffin cup of a mini muffin tin and lightly press it into the bottom and sides to form a cup. Cook the wontons from 4 to 5 minutes until the wontons are lightly browned.

To make the filling:

In a large skillet, cook the sausage until it is no longer pink. Remove the sausage to a bowl. Add the red peppers, cheese and mayonnaise and mix well. Fill each of the wonton cups with about 1 tablespoon of the filling. Bake for 6 to 7 minutes or until heated through. Garnish with parsley if desired.

Serve warm.

Baked Wonton Cups

Italian Sausage Wonton Appetizer

He who laughs last didn't get it.

Five Spice Ribs

These ribs are so good people eat them like candy. You can make an entire meal out of just these ribs! Everyone who has tried them says that they are addictive. Seldom are there any left over. As good as they are, they are a labor of love, but the result is worth the effort.

Ingredients:

- 1½ to 2 pounds meaty pork spareribs
- 3 tablespoons Kosher salt
- 1½ teaspoons Chinese Five-Spice powder
- 1½ teaspoon Szechwan pepper
- 1½ tablespoons cornstarch
- Wok or large saucepan ½ full of peanut oil

    Marinade:

- 2 tablespoons low sodium soy sauce
- 1 teaspoon sugar
- 2 tablespoons Chinese Rice Wine or Pale Dry Sherry
- ½ teaspoon freshly ground black pepper

First separate the rack into individual ribs. With a sharp heavy cleaver, cut the individual spareribs into 2" long pieces, or better still, have your butcher cut them up when you buy them. Most butchers won't charge you to run the ribs through the cutter, but you will still have to separate the pieces. Put the pieces in a bowl and set aside.

Add the salt and Szechwan pepper into a wok under medium heat and stir-fry (dry) for about 3 minutes or until the mixture starts to change color slightly. Remove from the wok and put in a small bowl. Mix in the Five-Spice powder and set aside to cool.

Sprinkle about ⅔ of the Five-Spice mixture over the ribs, and, using your hands, rub the mixture into the ribs making sure all are coated.

Make the marinade, add to the ribs and toss to coat them all evenly. Cover and refrigerate for 2 to 3 hours. Optimally, place all in a large zip-lock plastic bag.

Remove ribs from refrigerator. Discard any excess marinade. Sprinkle with the cornstarch and mix to cover evenly.

Put the peanut oil in the wok and heat the oil to about 350°. Deep-fry the ribs in small batches for about 3 minutes or until golden. Remove and set aside. Continue until all the ribs are done. Make sure the oil is back at 350° F and add all the ribs in at once. Cook for another 2 minutes, stirring the ribs around so they all are cooked until they turn a dark brown. Remove ribs to drain on paper towels. Sprinkle with the remaining Five-Spice powder to taste. Serve at once.

The customer in the Italian restaurant was so pleased with his meal that he asked to speak to the chef.

The owner proudly led him into the kitchen and introduced him to the chef.

"Your veal parmigiana was superb," the customer said. "I just spent a month in Italy, and yours is better than any I ever had over there."

"Naturally," the chef said. "Over there, they use domestic cheese. Ours is imported!"

Chinese Roast Pork Strips

Growing up in the Northeast, one of the favorite appetizers at Chinese restaurants was pork strips. It seems to be a regional dish and I do believe they were pre-cooked and then steamed before serving. Although this recipe isn't quite the same, it is actually more flavorful than the regional pork strips. The local joke was always trying to guess what the meat really was.

Ingredients:

- 2 pound pork tenderloin
- 2 tablespoons chicken stock
- 2 tablespoons soy sauce
- 1 teaspoon brown-bean sauce
- 1 tablespoon sherry
- 1½ tablespoons sugar
- 1 teaspoon salt
- 1 tablespoon of minced or finely chopped garlic
- 3 or 4 drops of red food coloring

Directions:

In a small bowl, combine the chicken stock, soy sauce, brown-bean sauce, sherry, sugar, salt, garlic and food coloring and stir until well mixed.

Pour the sauce into a large plastic airtight bag (1 gallon size works well) with the pork. Seal the bag, removing as much air as possible before sealing. Rotate the bag to coat all the pork. Allow to baste for 4 hours at room temperature or at least 6 hours to overnight in the refrigerator, turning the bag occasionally.

Preheat the oven to 350° F.

Place the pork in an oven rack placed in a roasting pan with about ½ inch of water to catch the drippings and prevent excessive smoking. Roast the pork for 45 minutes, and then raise the heat to 450° and cook for another 15 minutes. Let the pork rest for 5 minutes.

Slice the pork hot and serve with desired sauce such as Plum Sweet and Sour Sauce (see recipe).

Two fish swim into a concrete wall. One turns to the other and says "dam!"

Clams Casino

Clams Casino originated in Narragansett, Rhode Island, so they say, and is just a fancy name for clams on the half-shell with breadcrumbs and bacon. There are several ways to prepare this dish. Just remember, it's clams on the half-shell with breadcrumbs and bacon. That's what matters.

Ingredients:

- 24 large clams in shell or 12 Cherrystone clams, scrubbed
- 1 green bell pepper, medium sized, finely diced
- 1 red bell pepper, medium sized, finely diced
- 2 shallots, chopped
- 2 cloves garlic, minced
- 1/3 cup bread crumbs (plain or flavored as desired)
- ½ teaspoon kosher salt
- ½ teaspoon freshly ground pepper
- 1/3 cup white wine
- 1 tablespoon olive oil
- 3 slices bacon cut into 1 inch pieces for large clams (12), 1½ inches for Cherrystones (6)

Directions:

Heat the oil in a heavy large skillet over medium heat. Add the bell peppers, shallots, garlic, salt, pepper and sauté until the shallots are tender and translucent, about 5 minutes. Add the wine and simmer until it is almost evaporated, about 2 minutes. Remove the skillet from the heat and let cool completely.

While the vegetable filling is cooling, make sure the clams are scrubbed and clean. Discard the clams with broken shells or clams that are opened. Steam the clams for about five minutes until the clams open up. Drain the clams, reserving the clam broth for other recipes if desired. Make sure all the clams have opened. Discard any clams that do not open, they are not edible. When cool enough to handle, break off the top half of each clam (the part that doesn't have the clam meat) and discard. With a sharp knife, cut the clam meat free from the shell; leave the meat in the half shell. If you are using large Cherrystones, you may opt to cut up the clam meat into smaller pieces. You may mix it with the vegetable filling mixture at this point if desired, but make sure that the clam meat is evenly distributed in each clamshell when filling.

Clams Casino

Take each clam half shell and put the vegetable mixture on top of the clams. Don't pack it tightly. Sprinkle breadcrumbs to cover the entire top of each shell. Top each shell with a generous piece of the bacon large enough to cover most of the shell (remember that the bacon will shrink to about half the original size). Place all the clams on a baking sheet and into a broiler in the middle rack position and broil until the bacon is cooked. Serve hot, top with a dash of lemon juice if desired.

A vulture boards an airplane, carrying two dead raccoons. The Flight Attendant looks at him and says, 'I'm sorry, sir, only one carrion allowed per passenger."

Poached Shimp Cocktail

DON'T BOIL THAT SHRIMP!!

If you have always boiled your shrimp for shrimp cocktail or other simple shrimp recipes, you are cooking away flavor and giving the shrimp a tough texture. Poaching shrimp is easy, foolproof and adds enormous flavor and a tender texture to North America's favorite seafood. Here is a basic recipe for poaching shrimp. It can be altered to create the taste you desire. Try eating a plain shrimp after you cook it this way, you may find that you don't need cocktail sauce.

Ingredients:

- 1-pound large raw shrimp (I like to use 16-21 count)
- 3 cups water
- 1 cup white wine
- 1 large lemon
- 1 medium onion
- 2 cloves of garlic or more if desired
- 1 large Bay Leaf
- 2 teaspoons Kosher or Sea Salt

Directions:

Peel and devein the shrimp. You may leave the tail either on or off. Save the shells to add to the poaching liquid if desired.

To make the poaching liquid, add the water and wine to a medium saucepan. Thinly slice the onion and garlic and add to the liquid. Zest the lemon, juice the lemon and add both to the liquid. Add the bay leaf, salt and the shrimp shells. Bring the liquid to a simmer.

Simmer the liquid until it becomes aromatic (about 5 minutes), then add the shrimp, cover the saucepan and **turn off** the heat. Let it sit for 10 minutes. While the shrimp is sitting, take a medium to large bowl and fill it with ice water.

After the 10 minutes, remove just the shrimp and place them in the ice water to stop the cooking. You can discard the poaching liquid.

The shrimp may be served at once or refrigerated for several days.

Tips:

Be adventurous with your tastes for the poaching liquid. You may add whatever spices you desire, such as peppercorns, Old Bay seasoning, saffron, celery or whatever. The only required ingredients are the water, wine, and salt. Everything else is your choice.

Poached Shrimp in Poaching Liquid

Poached Shrimp Cocktail

A man spies a letter lying on his doormat. It says "DO NOT BEND"
He spends the next 2 hours trying to figure out how to pick it up.

Coconut Shrimp

These are so good, pretty to look at, and easy to make. One of the good things about them is that you make them a bit ahead of time and refrigerate before cooking, which eliminates the rush-rush of trying to do multiple dishes at the same time.

Ingredients:

- 1 egg
- ½ cup flour
- ¾ cup beer*
- 1½ teaspoons baking powder
- 2 cups flaked coconut
- ¼ cup flour for dredging
- 24 16-20 count shrimp, peeled and deveined, tails on

Directions:

Line a baking sheet with waxed paper.

Place ¼ cup of flour and the coconut in two separate bowls.

In medium bowl, mix the egg, ½ cup flour, the beer and baking powder until smooth.

Hold shrimp by the tail, and dredge in flour, shaking off excess flour. Dip in egg/beer batter; allow excess to drip off. Roll each shrimp in the coconut, pressing the coconut gently to help adhere it to the shrimp and then place each on the baking sheet. Refrigerate for at least 30 minutes. The refrigeration allows the beer batter to firm up holding the coconut in place when frying.

Heat the oil to 350° F in a deep fryer. Fry shrimp in batches of no more than 6 each, cook, turning once, for 2 to 3 minutes, or until golden brown. Try to maintain the oil temp at 350. The temp will dip down every time you add new shrimp. Remove shrimp to paper towels to drain. Serve warm with your favorite dipping sauce.

* Make sure you use a beer with a good flavor. Weak or light beers will not be as good.

Coconut Shrimp

TIP:

With all fried food, it is important to keep the oil temperature as close to the original set temperature as possible. Therefore, fry foods in small batches since the oil temperature will go down initially whenever you add food to the oil. The more you add, the lower the temperature will go and thus the longer food has to sit in the oil before the temperature rises, allowing more oil to be absorbed into the food causing a heavier, greasier end product.

Creamy Shrimp Dip in Wonton Cups

Here is another wonton cup appetizer that is delicious and impressive for guest. It is very easy to make and both the wontons and the filling can be made ahead of time.

Ingredients:

- 1 pound large cooked, peeled, and deveined shrimp, chopped
- 2 green onions, finely chopped
- ¼ – ½ shallot, finely chopped (depending on size)
- 1/3 cup mayonnaise
- 1/3 cup sour cream
- 2 tablespoons fresh tarragon leaves, finely chopped
- 2 teaspoons rice vinegar
- ½ teaspoon Kosher salt
- ¼ teaspoon freshly ground black pepper
- 24 wontons cups (see below)
- **Garnish: fresh chives (optional)**

Directions:

To make the dip:

Place the shrimp, onion, shallot, mayonnaise, sour cream, tarragon and rice vinegar, pepper and ¼ teaspoon of salt in a medium bowl and combine well. Cover the bowl and refrigerate for from 30 minutes to one day.
Fill each of the wonton cups with about 1 tablespoon for the dip. Garnish with chives if desired.

To make the wonton cups:

Preheat the oven to 350°.
Put a wonton in each cup of a mini muffin tin to form the cup top side up. Cook the wontons from 3 to 4 minutes until the wontons are firm and keep their shape. If desired, bake until they are golden brown and skip the deep frying, or remove and let cool, then deep fry the wontons in a fryer at 350° until golden brown, just a minute or two. Remove to drain on a paper towel and salt lightly. Let cool completely before filling.

Serve chilled.

Creamy Shrimp Dip in Wonton Cups

A couple of clams were eating chocolate bars while two fish watched.

"Did you see that?" one fish said, as the clams finished their treat.

"They didn't offer us a single bite!"

"What do you expect?" asked the other fish. "They're two shellfish."

Drunken Shrimp

This shrimp dish makes a fantastic addition to any cookout or party. Just stir-fry them on the stove when the time is right. These can also be cooked on the grill.

Ingredients:

- ¼ cup brandy
- 1 pound medium shrimp, shelled and deveined
- Salt and freshly ground pepper
- ¼ cup vegetable oil

Directions:

In a shallow dish, add the brandy to the shrimp; marinate for 15 to 30 minutes.

Remove the shrimp from the marinade and drain lightly on paper towels. Season with salt and pepper

In a large skillet, heat 2 tablespoons of the oil until simmering. Add half of the shrimp and stir-fry over high heat until browned on both sides and cooked through, about 1 minute total. Transfer to a platter and repeat with the remaining shrimp. Serve immediately.

Saw a man standing on one leg at an ATM.
Confused, I asked him what he was doing?
He said he was just checking his balance.

Italian Fried Shrimp

This is another tasty shrimp dish that can be used as an appetizer or as a main dish with sides. You can experiment with different types or combinations of grated cheeses.

Ingredients:

- 1 pound raw shrimp, shelled and deveined tail on or off, (I use 16-20 count)
- 1/3 cup flour
- 2 eggs
- 1 tablespoon milk
- 1/3 cup Italian Style Breadcrumbs
- ½ cup grated Pecorino Romano cheese
- 1 tablespoon basil
- 1 tablespoon oregano
- 1 ½ teaspoons thyme
- 3 tablespoons olive oil
- 2 tablespoon butter
- 1 teaspoon salt
- 1 teaspoon pepper

Directions:

Poach the shrimp as in the Poached Shrimp Cocktail recipe; go a bit heavy on the garlic. Use right away or you may refrigerate to use at a later date.

Use 3 deep dishes. In the first place the flour. Add the salt and pepper and mix to combine. In the second dish add the eggs and the milk. Whisk until well blended. In the third dish, add the breadcrumbs, cheese, basil, oregano and thyme, mix until well combined.

One at a time, dredge each of the shrimps in the flour and well covered; shake off any excess. Then dredge each the shrimp in the egg mixture and coat completely letting any excess drip off back into the dish. Now put the shrimp in the breadcrumb mixture and coat completely, pressing the shrimp into the mixture to make sure the mixture adheres well. Place the coated shrimp on a place and do the next one. Continue until all the shrimp are done. You can start to cook immediately or place the shrimps in the refrigerator for up to 30 minutes before cooking.

Heat a medium sized skillet over medium-high heat; add the oil and butter. Once the butter has completely melted place about 1/3 of the shrimps in the skillet and cook for 1 to 2 minutes, just until the cooked side turn golden brown. Turn them over and cook until the bottoms are also golden brown. Don't forget that the shrimp are already cooked, so you only need to brown the outside. They will still be plenty hot when done. Carefully remove the shrimps to a dish or serving platter. Continue cooking until all the shrimp are done. Allow the shrimps to cool, to allow the breading to adhere to the shrimp, before serving.

Italian Fried Shrimp

Census Taker: "How many children do you have?"

Woman: "Four."

"Census Taker: "May I have their names, please?"

Woman: "Eenee, Meenee, Minee and George."

Census Taker: "Okay, that's fine. But may I ask why you named your fourth child George?"

Woman: "Because we didn't want any Moe!

Crispy Fried Shrimp, Chinese Style

If you like your fried shrimp golden and crispy then this is the recipe for you.
It's better than you get at most restaurants, which give you a lot of batter
with a small shrimp. These have way more shrimp than batter.

Ingredients:

- 1 pound raw shrimp, 16-20 count works best
- 1 egg, beaten
- 1 tablespoon cornstarch
- 1 teaspoon sherry
- ½ teaspoon soy sauce
- ¼ teaspoon salt
- Oil for frying

Batter:

- ½ cup all-purpose flour
- ½ cup chicken stock or water
- 3 tablespoons cornstarch
- 1 tablespoon vegetable oil
- ½ teaspoon baking soda
- ½ teaspoon salt

Directions:

Peel and devein the shrimp leaving the tails on if desired. Blend the egg, 1 tablespoon of cornstarch, wine, soy sauce and ¼ teaspoon of salt in a bowl. Stir in the shrimp to coat then place in the refrigerator for 10 minutes.

Heat the oil in a large saucepan, wok, or deep fryer to 375° F. In a bowl, mix the flour, chicken stock, cornstarch, and the tablespoon of oil, the baking soda and salt. Add the shrimp and gently stir until coated. Fry no more than 6 shrimp at a time, turning occasionally, until golden brown, about 2 to 3 minutes. Drain. Serve hot with the dipping sauce of your choice.

I'm reading a book about anti-gravity. It's impossible to put down.

Cold Ginger Shrimp

Do you think I like shrimp recipes? Maybe it's because when I buy shrimp,
it's sometimes in 4-pound blocks (it's less expensive that way).
And what do you do with 4 pounds of shrimp once it has been thawed?
Why, you find a lot of shrimp recipes, of course. This is another do-ahead recipe.

Ingredients:

- 1 ½ pounds raw shrimp (16 to 24 count size works best)
  (See what I mean ... now I have 2 ½ pounds left!)
- 4 cups water
- 2 tablespoons salt

Marinade:

- ¼ cup soy sauce
- 3 tablespoons finely chopped gingerroot
- ¼ cup white vinegar
- 2 tablespoons sugar
- 2 tablespoons of a sweet white wine
- 1 ½ teaspoons salt
- 1-2 scallions thinly sliced for garnish

Directions:

Peel and devein the shrimp. Heat the water to boiling and add the 2 tablespoons of salt and the shrimp. Cover and heat to boiling, reduce heat and let simmer for about 2 minutes more. Drain. Or, better still, poach the shrimp as in the poached shrimp recipe to add more flavor.

Heat the soy sauce to boiling, then add the gingerroot; reduce the heat to simmer and simmer until most of the liquid is absorbed. Stir in the vinegar, sugar, wine and 1½ teaspoons of salt. Place the shrimp in a large sealable plastic bag and pour in the marinade mixture. Seal the bag, eliminating as much air as possible, and rotate the contents to coat all the shrimp. Refrigerate for 3 to 4 hours. To serve, remove the shrimp from the marinade and place on a platter; sprinkle with the scallions.

HOT AND COLD SHRIMP
Crispy Fried Shrimp (left) and Ginger Shrimp (right) with
Plum Sweet and Sour Dipping Sauce

"The odds of going to the store for a loaf of bread and coming out with only a loaf of bread are three billion to one." - Erma Bombeck

Braised Garlic Shrimp and Scallops

Here's another use for some of that shrimp that is left over. I use weights for the scallops and shrimp in this recipe, but what I really do is buy one or two very large scallops and shrimp per person.

Ingredients:

- ½ pound 16/20 count shrimp
- ½ pound large Sea Scallops
- ¼ cup Olive oil
- 4 Garlic cloves, minced
- ¼ cup dry white wine
- 2 tablespoons butter
- Salt
- Pepper

Optional:
- 1/3 cup Parsley, chopped
- Lemon wedges

Directions:

Shell and devein shrimp, leave the tails on if desired. Wash the shrimp and scallops under cold running water and pat dry with paper towels. Heat a large skillet over medium heat. When the skillet is hot, add the oil, garlic and the butter. Sauté for about 1 minute being careful not to let the garlic burn. Place the scallops in the skillet, one at a time, flat side down. Space them about 1 inch apart. Once they are in the skillet do not move them. Now add the shrimp to the skillet so that they are not overlapping. Cook for about 2 minutes. The Scallops should be a nice golden brown on the cooked side. Turn the shrimp and scallops over and cook for another 2 minutes.

Plate the shrimp and scallops. Add the wine to the skillet and deglaze the liquid for about 1 minute then add the parsley and continue to cook for another ½ minute. Pour the liquid over the plated seafood. Serve immediately with lemon wedges.

Braised Garlic Shrimp and Scallops

It's a 5 minute walk from my house to the pub.

It's a 35 minute walk from the pub to my house.

The difference is staggering.

Shrimp and Pork Egg Rolls

Shrimp eggs rolls are what started me on Oriental cooking. The memory stemmed from of all those shrimp egg rolls we used to eat at the drive-in theaters in the late '60's and early '70's in those days when they still had drive in theaters. Those egg rolls were very greasy and probably had absolutely no shrimp in them at all. Nutritional value was nil. But, we would spend more money on shrimp egg rolls than everything else combined, including ticket price and gas.

Now these egg rolls, on the other hand, are better than you will get at any restaurant. These are quite filling and can be used as a main dish. Many a time, the whole family would show up for a dinner of shrimp egg rolls. This recipe will make about 16 large egg rolls. All my kids have always loved these. I do this recipe as a two-day event. Make the filling on day one and do the cooking on day two.

Ingredients:

- 8 to 12 ounces of fresh bean sprouts
- ½ pound of fresh uncooked shrimp
- ½ pound of lean pork, ground
- 3 cups of finely diced celery
- 4 or 5 medium sized fresh mushrooms cut into ¼ inch slices
- 3 tablespoons of peanut oil
- 2 tablespoons of soy sauce
- 2 tablespoons of rice wine or cooking sherry (pale dry)
- 3 teaspoons of salt
- 1 teaspoon of sugar
- 2 tablespoon of cornstarch dissolved in 3 tablespoons of cold water
- 1 or 2 packages of pre-made egg roll wrappers (depending on count) available at most grocery stores.
- 2 - 4 cups peanut oil for cooking assembled egg rolls.
- Lightly beaten egg, milk or water to seal wrappers.

Directions:

Part 1: Making the filling.

Put the bean sprouts in a large bowl. Fill with cold water and discard any of the green husks that float to the top. Drain and pat dry with paper towels.

Clean, shell and devein the shrimp. Dice them using a sharp knife or cleaver, but not too small.

In a cup, add the wine, soy sauce and sugar and set aside.

Put in a tablespoon of oil in the wok, make sure all the sides are coated and turn the heat up to high. When the oil starts to smoke, add the pork and lower the heat to medium high. Stir-fry the pork until it is no longer pink. Add the wine/soy mixture, shrimp and mushrooms and continue to stir-fry until the all the shrimp turn pink. Transfer entire contents of wok into a large bowl and set aside.

Prepared Shrimp, Mushrooms and Pork filling.

Put the last 2 tablespoons of oil in the wok and swish around until the oil is hot and starts to smoke. Add the celery and stir-fry for about five minutes. Add the salt and bean sprouts and mix thoroughly. Return the pork/shrimp mixture and cook, stirring constantly, until the liquid at the bottom of the wok starts to boil. Be careful not to overcook. You don't want the sprouts to get soggy.

There should not be more than a few tablespoons of liquid in the bottom of the wok. If there is more, use a large spoon to discard it. Give the cornstarch and water mixture a stir to recombine them. Part the contents of the wok so that the liquid is exposed in the bottom of the wok. Slowly add the cornstarch mixture and stir continually until the liquid thickens. Mix the contents thoroughly until everything is coated. Transfer entire contents to a large bowl to let cool.

Set aside to cool to room temperature or cover with plastic wrap and refrigerate overnight.

Part 2: Filling the wrappers, cooking and eating!

If refrigerated, discard all the liquid but a couple of tablespoons that has settled; take out the filling and give it a stir to reintroduce the liquid that is left. Let sit until at room temperature and then drain any liquid at the bottom of the bowl. This is important because if the filling is too wet, it will soften the wrappers and even make holes in them not to mention splatter when it hits the hot oil.

To fill each egg roll, take a single wrapper and place in front of you with one of the corners pointing toward you forming a diamond shape (see photographs, below). Using a fork and your fingers, place 2 - 3 tablespoons of the filling (use your own discretion on how much to use) in a horizontal line about ¼ the way up the wrapper. The filling should come to about an inch from each edge. Now take the flap pointing toward you and wrap it over the filling, tucking the point under the filling. Now roll the wrapper and filling to the halfway point of the wrapper. Using a lightly beaten egg, milk or water, brush (I uses my fingers) the exposed edges of the triangle of the wrapper. Fold the left and right points over the middle and roll the wrapper to close. The egg/water/milk will seal the wrapper closed. Continue until all the egg rolls are done. Cover with a damp towel until ready to cook.

1. Position wrapper with point toward you. Place filling on wrapper.

2. Fold lower corner over and tuck under filling.

3. Fold over left and right corners.

4. Roll egg roll to close the package.

To cook, put the peanut oil in a wok or deep fryer and heat to 375° F. Place 2 to four egg rolls in the oil making sure that they are completely covered in the oil. Fry for about four minutes until golden brown. Place on cooling rack or extra layers of paper towels to drain while you cook the next batch. Serve as soon as possible with your favorite duck or plum sauce. We eat them with our hands. Take the first bite off the end, exposing the insides then spoon in the sauce and let it seep in.

Shrimp and Pork Egg Rolls

Fried Calamari

Fried calamari is another of my favorite appetizers. It was hard to find a breading or batter that was just right. After trying more recipes than I can remember, this is the one I like the best.

Ingredients:

- ¼ cup all purpose flour
- ½ cup cornstarch
- ½ cup corn flour (not corn meal, although you may opt for it)
- 2 teaspoon sea salt
- 1 teaspoon crushed black peppercorns
- ½ teaspoon cayenne pepper (or to taste)
- 2 cups buttermilk
- 1 quart vegetable or peanut oil
- 1 pound cleaned calamari, bodies cut into ½ inch thick rings, tentacles halved

Directions:

Soak the calamari in the buttermilk for 20 to 30 minutes.

In a large saucepan or deep fryer, heat the vegetable oil to 375° F.

In a bowl, whisk the flours, cornstarch, salt, pepper and cayenne until well blended and set aside.

Drain the buttermilk from the calamari.

Set a wire rack over a baking sheet. Working in batches, add the calamari to the dry mix and mix until the calamari is evenly covered inside and out. Using a large gauge strainer, shake off the extra dry mix and gently drop into the hot oil. Use a frying screen to prevent the oil from splattering. Continue adding the calamari to different parts of the saucepan until the whole batch has been added. Fry the calamari over high heat until deep golden, about 2 minutes. Using a slotted spoon, transfer the calamari to the rack. Repeat for the remaining 4 batches.

Serve at once with lemon or Simple Marinara Sauce (see recipe).

Fried Calamari with Simple Marinara Sauce

A thief broke into the local police station and stole all the lavatory equipment.
A spokesperson was quoted as saying, "We have absolutely nothing to go on."

Crab Wontons

This is such an awesome appetizer. It seems like a lot of work, but it is really simple, and the filling takes just minutes to prepare. The wontons, once wrapped, can be refrigerated for several hours before being cooked.

The recipe calls for one can of crabmeat. This is for ease of use. But, if you go to your local fish monger and buy a good quality fresh crabmeat (more expensive), the end product is all that much better.

Ingredients:

- 1 package of pre-made Won-Ton wrappers (available at most grocers)
- 1 can (8 ounces) crabmeat (lump is the best), drained
- 3 scallions, finely chopped
- 1/3 cup chopped water chestnuts
- 8 ounces soft cream cheese
- 1 tablespoon soy sauce
- Milk for sealing the wrappers
- Peanut oil for frying
- Optional: 1 clove garlic, minced

Directions:

Drain the crabmeat. Mix the crabmeat, cream cheese, scallions, water chestnuts, and soy sauce in a bowl until well combined.

Place about 1 small teaspoon of the mixture in the center of each wonton wrapper. Brush the top 2 edges of the wrapper with the milk and fold one corner of the wonton wrapper over the filling to the opposite corner to form a triangle (see photographs). Press the edges to seal. Brush the right or left corner with the egg or milk and bring the two corners together below the filling and pinch together to seal. Repeat this with all the wontons. To keep them from drying out, place them under a damp towel.

Place filling in center of wrapper

Fold over corner to form triangle.

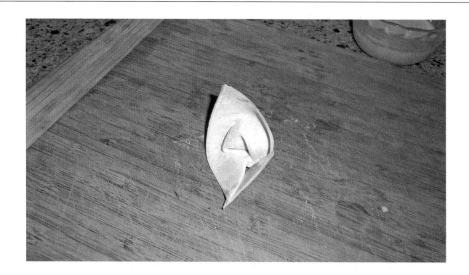

Wrap corners on long end together bending the center of the Won Ton

Heat about 2 inches of oil in a large saucepan, wok or deep fryer to 350° F. Fry about 6 wontons at a time, turning several times, until golden brown, about 3 minutes. Remove and drain. Serve with dipping sauce of your choice.

Crab Won Tons on pretty oriental plate with dipping sauce

Steamed Mussels

I first discovered steamed mussels on a business trip to Germany many years ago. The small group I was with loved them so much we kept ordering them until the restaurant ran out.

For each recipe, first wash the mussels thoroughly, pulling off any pieces of protruding beard.

To cook the mussels base recipe:

Simmer desired ingredients for about 5 minutes, then add the mussels, cover the pot, and turn the heat up to high. When steam starts to shoot out from under the lid, turn the heat back down to medium. Leave the pot on the heat for 5 minutes more.

Leave the lid on the pot and holding down the lid with a kitchen towel. Shake pot to redistribute the mussels. Put the pot back on the heat for 2 minutes more. Take off the lid and check to see if all the mussels have opened. If not, replace the lid and cook for 2 minutes more.

Remove the lid, wait a minute for the steam to dissipate, scoop the mussels out of the pot with a large slotted spoon, and place them in hot bowls, discarding any unopened mussels. If the liquid in the bottom of the pan is sandy, carefully pour it into a clean saucepan, leaving any sand or grit behind, and then pour over the mussels.

Serve either recipe with fresh crusty Italian or French bread to mop up the juices.

Simple Steamed Mussels with wine:

- 2 dozen mussels
- ½ cup white wine
- 4 cloves garlic, minced
- 1 small onion, thinly sliced
- Parsley

In large pot, heat the wine. Add garlic, onion, and parsley. Cook the mussels as above. Pour broth over mussels and serve.

Not-So-Simple Steamed Mussels with wine:

- 6 pounds mussels, preferably small cultivated

- 2 cups dry white wine
- 3 shallots, finely chopped
- 1 bay leaf
- 2 fresh thyme sprigs or ½ teaspoon dried thyme
- 3 tablespoons finely chopped parsley
- ¼ pound unsalted butter (optional)
- Pepper

Combine the wine, shallots, bay leaf, and thyme in a 10-quart pot and bring to a simmer over medium heat. Cook the mussels as above. After the mussels are removed, add the chopped parsley to the hot broth, whisk in the butter if desired, and season with pepper. Heat the broth for 1 or 2 minutes to reduce the liquid by half and ladle it over the hot mussels and serve.

Steamed Mussels and crusty bread for dipping

I went to a seafood disco last week and pulled a mussel.

Fried Lobster

Why would anyone take wonderful lobster meat and fry it?
Because it's really good, that's why!

Ingredients:

- 1 Maine Lobster 1½ -2 pounds
- 2 tablespoons sherry
- 1 tablespoon oyster or soy sauce
- 2 slices fresh ginger root, minced
- 2 eggs
- 4 tablespoons cornstarch
- 2 tablespoons water
- ½ teaspoon salt
- Oil for deep frying
- Lettuce
- Pepper

Directions:

Boil or steam the lobster until cooked, then shell it and extract the meat. Cut the meat in 1 to 2 inch pieces.

Marinate the lobster meat in a mixture of the sherry, oyster or soy sauce, and ginger root. Let stand 30 minutes, tossing cubes occasionally; then drain, discarding marinade.

Beat eggs lightly and add the cornstarch, water, and salt. Beat into a smooth batter. Dip lobster pieces in the batter to coat.

Heat the oil to 375° F in a deep fryer or deep saucepan. Add coated lobster pieces, a few at a time, and deep-fry for about ½ minute or until golden. Drain on paper toweling.

Arrange lobster on a bed of shredded lettuce, sprinkle with pepper and serve.

Serves 4.

Fried Lobster

Evidence has been found that William Tell and his family were avid bowlers.
However, all the league records were unfortunately destroyed in a fire.
Thus we'll never know for whom the Tells bowled.

Yakatori/Kushiyaki

In Japanese cuisine, Kushiyaki refers to all foods that are skewered and grilled, including beef, chicken, pork, seafood and vegetables. Yakatori means skewered chicken (vegetables and chicken) grilled over an open flame. In the West, this term has been adopted to refer to almost anything that is skewered and grilled.

Ingredients:

- 1 pound beef flank steak, chicken or whatever you desire, thinly sliced
- ½ cup sugar
- 2/3 cup soy sauce
- 2 tablespoons sake
- 1 small piece grated ginger (about 1 teaspoon)
- 1 - 2 cloves crushed garlic
- 2 tablespoons sesame seeds (add more to taste)
- 2 tablespoons canola oil
- 2 stalks chopped green onions
- Bamboo skewers

Directions:

Soak the skewers in water for at least a couple of hours. Alternatively use metal skewers.

Combine the soy sauce, sake, oil, lemon juice, sesame seeds, sugar, green onions, garlic, and ginger in a large secure container or re-sealable plastic storage bag. Mix or shake the ingredients well and refrigerate.

Slice the steak into thin 2 inch by 2 inch pieces and marinate in the prepared marinade for at least 2 hours. Marinating the meat for over 4 hours will result in the meat being overly salty due to the soy sauce.

Thread several pieces of the meat onto each skewer. Discard the left over marinade

Preheat the grill/broiler for medium to high heat, and position the grate 5 inches from coals/burner. Cook to desired wellness, about 3 minutes per side. Because the meat is sliced thinly, it cooks fairly quickly.

Old cooks never die, they just get deranged.

Tomato Salsa

This is a great dipping salsa and is also what is used in the fajita recipe (see recipe).

Ingredients:

- 3 Tomatoes medium sized
- 1 jalapeño pepper
- ½ medium sized red onion finely chopped
- ½ teaspoon sugar
- 3 tablespoons olive oil
- Juice from 1 lime
- ½ bunch of cilantro chopped
- ½ clove garlic, chopped (optional)
- Salt and fresh ground pepper

Directions:

Slice the tomatoes first and then chop them taking out the seeds. Deseed and finely chop the pepper. Make sure you wash your hands after chopping since the pepper is an eye irritant.

Mix the onion, the green pepper, garlic (if desired), and the cilantro with the tomatoes. Squeeze the lime juice and pour over the vegetables in the bowl. Add the olive oil, salt and pepper. Blend all the ingredients together, until well mixed. Taste the salsa and add salt and pepper to taste.

Serve or refrigerate.

Tomato Salsa

Tangy Hot Dog Appetizers

This is a simple good tasting eat-it-with-toothpicks appetizer. This is another good one that is made ahead of time to free you up to do other last minute dishes.

Ingredients:

- 1 pound all-beef frankfurters cut into 1 inch pieces or 1 pound cocktail franks
- 4 tablespoons butter
- 1/3 cup chopped onion
- ½ cup water
- ½ cup ketchup
- ¼ cup vinegar
- 2 tablespoons Worcestershire Sauce
- 1 tablespoon prepared mustard
- ¼ cup brown sugar
- ¼ teaspoon salt
- 1/8 teaspoon pepper
- A large quantity of toothpicks

Directions:

Heat a large skillet over medium high heat and add the butter. When melted, add the onions and sauté for 1 minute. Stir in the rest of the ingredients and bring to a boil. Pour the sauce into a crock-pot or large saucepan and add the franks and baste with the sauce. Let the contents cook on the high setting for at least 30 minutes. Serve hot with toothpicks right from the crock-pot or put in a heated bowl.

There are only 3 types of people in the world, those who can count, and those who can't.

Fried Mushrooms

You can get them in restaurants, so why not make them yourself?

Ingredients:

- 10 ounces fresh white mushrooms
- 1 cup all-purpose flour
- ½ cup cornstarch
- ¾ teaspoon baking powder
- ¼ teaspoon salt
- 1 cup water
- 2 cups breadcrumbs (plain, seasoned, or Panko as desired)

Directions:

Clean the mushrooms and set aside.

Mix the flour, baking powder and salt in a bowl. Add the water to make a batter and mix until smooth. Dip the clean mushrooms into the batter to cover. Let excess batter drip off. You might wish to use toothpicks or skewers to make the dipping easier. After dipping the mushrooms, roll them in the desired breadcrumbs to coat. Deep fry at 375° F until golden brown.

Serve plain or with dipping or cocktail sauce. For ease of use, serve with toothpicks.

Fried Mushrooms

Pencils could be made with erasers at both ends, but what would be the point?

ENTREES

Aloha Chicken

Beef With Oyster Sauce

A nice, very flavorful main dish that is simple yet elegant. One of the few dishes that tastes just as good the 2nd day, that is, if there is any left the first day! This is another one of my favorite recipes.

Ingredients:

- 1 pound beef steak; sirloin, flank or any flavorful steak cut

Marinade:
- 1½ tablespoons dark soy sauce
- 1 tablespoon Chinese rice wine or dry sherry
- 2 teaspoons cornstarch
- 1½ tablespoons water
- 1 tablespoon vegetable oil

Other:
- ¼ -inch slice ginger, chopped
- ¾ cup sliced mushrooms
- 1 small carrot, peeled and cut diagonally into thin slices
- 2½ tablespoons oyster sauce
- ½ teaspoon granulated or soft brown sugar
- ¼ cup low-sodium chicken broth
- 4 tablespoons oil for stir-frying, or as needed
- Salt and pepper, to taste

Directions:

Cut the beef across the grain into thin slices, 2 – 3-inches long and no more than ¼-inch thick. Add the marinade ingredients in the order given. Marinate the beef for 15 minutes. In a small bowl, mix the chicken broth, sugar and oyster sauce together and set aside.

Heat 2 tablespoons oil in the wok over medium-high to high heat.

Add the ginger and stir-fry quickly until aromatic. Add the beef. Stir-fry until it changes color and is nearly cooked through. (Cook the beef in several batches if needed). Remove the beef slices from the wok and drain. Clean out the wok.

Beef with Oyster Sauce on Rice

Heat 2 tablespoons oil in the wok. Add the sliced carrot, stir-fry briefly then add the mushrooms. Push the vegetables to the side and add the sauce in the middle. Let come to a boil, and then add the beef back into the pan. Mix everything together - taste and adjust seasoning if desired. Serve hot with steamed rice.

Serves 4.

"My doctor told me I had to stop throwing intimate dinners for four unless there are three other people." -Orson Welles

Roast Beef Cooking

Various cuts of meat take different amounts of time to cook. In an ideal world, everyone would have a thermometer — either an instant-read thermometer or a meat thermometer that stays in the roast the whole time it's cooking. Then you would know that the roast is done when the temperature in the center of the roast reaches 120°F to 125°F, (49°C to 52°C) for rare, 130°F to 140°F (55°C to 60°C) for medium rare, 145°F to 150°F (63°C to 66°C) for medium, and 155°F to 165°F (68°C to 74°C) for well done.

Without a meat thermometer, you're taking a bit of a gamble. The size and shape of the meat, the amount of fat and bone, how the meat was aged and other factors affect how long it should cook.

Cooking at an oven temperature of 300°F (149°C), a 5- to 8-lb standing rib roast will take 17-19 minutes per pound for rare, 20-22 for medium rare, 23-25 minutes for medium, and 27-30 minutes for well done. A sirloin roast of 8- to 12-lbs will take 16-20 minutes for rare, 20-22 for medium rare, 23-25 for medium, and 26-30 for well done. A boneless top round, by contrast, will take 28-30 minutes for rare, 30-33 for medium rare, 34-38 for medium, and 40-45 for well done.

The higher the cooking temperature you use the greater the variation in doneness of the meat. Cooking at 300°F (149°C) will provide in a medium rare center, but more well done on the outer parts. I cook my roasts at 200°F (93°C) and allow 50 minutes per pound. That gives a consistent doneness throughout the entire roast (medium-rare) like you would get in a high quality restaurant, but I still use the thermometer.

After the roast comes out of the oven, let it rest for 15 to 20 minutes, which allows the juices to become more evenly distributed within the meat and makes it easier to carve. The temperature of the roast will rise 5° to 10° after you take it from the oven, so if you are using a thermometer, you should take it out a bit before it reaches the desired temperature.

Or forget all that stuff above and use the following instead:

Gracie Allen's Classic Recipe for Roast Beef

Ingredients:
1 large Roast of beef
1 small Roast of beef
Directions:
Take the two roasts and put them in the oven.
When the little one burns, the big one is done.

Oven Roasted Barbecue Brisket

If you love barbecue brisket but don't have a smoker, try this simple alternative that tastes just like the smoked barbeque brisket you get at barbecue eateries. To make it even better, try adding a little liquid smoke to add that authentic smoke flavor.

Ingredients:

- 1 4 to 5 pound beef brisket, trimmed
- ½ cup packed brown sugar
- 3 tablespoons Worcestershire Sauce
- 4 cloves garlic, minced
- 2 tablespoon chili powder
- 2 tablespoon ground black pepper
- 1 tablespoon yellow mustard
- 1 teaspoon salt
- 1 teaspoon cumin
- ¼ teaspoon nutmeg

Directions:

Combine all the ingredients except the brisket in a bowl. Mix well. Rub over all surfaces of the brisket to completely cover the meat. Wrap tightly in aluminum foil and place in the refrigerator over night.

Preheat the oven to 300° F. Place the brisket on a roasting rack in a roasting pan. Put several holes in the top of the foil to allow the steam to escape while cooking. Cook for 4 hours or until the internal temperature of the meat reaches 165° F. Remove brisket from the foil and let rest for at least 10 minutes before slicing and serving. Serve with your favorite barbeque sauce, like Rudy's (see recipe), either plated or in a sandwich.

Barbequed brisket is a low and slow cooked meat, so alternatively, you may preheat the oven to just 200° F and cook for 6 hours. But the important thing is the internal temperature of the meat should be around 165° F. Use a meat thermometer to gauge the temperature.

This brisket is great with Rudy's Barbeque Sauce (see recipe).

He had a photographic memory, which was never developed.

Mongolian Beef

Who ever thought that just beef and onions could taste so good? An historical note: This recipe has nothing to do with Mongolian cooking. It was just a name given to make the dish sound exotic.

Ingredients:

- 1 pound flank steak
- 1/3 cup water
- 2 tablespoons rice wine, dry white wine or the like
- 1 tablespoon Hoisin sauce
- 1 tablespoon soy sauce
- 1 tablespoon hot bean sauce or ½ teaspoon of ground red pepper
- 2 teaspoons cornstarch
- 1 teaspoon sesame oil (optional, but nice to use)
- 1 tablespoon cooking oil/peanut oil for stir-frying (use more if needed)
- 2+ cloves garlic, minced (to taste)
- 10 to 12 green onions bias sliced into 1 inch pieces or 1 large or 2 medium yellow onions cut into 1 inch squares or wedges

Directions:

Thinly slice the meat across the grain into bite sized strips. Partially freezing the meat may make this easier.

Make the sauce. In a small bowl stir together the water, wine, Hoisin sauce, bean sauce or red pepper, corn starch, soy sauce and sesame oil. Set aside.

Pour the oil into wok and swish around to coat. Heat to medium high. Stir-fry the garlic for about 15-30 seconds. Add the onions and stir-fry until tender. Remove and set aside.

Add a small portion of the beef to the wok and cook 2 or 3 minutes. Remove from the wok and repeat until all the beef is done.

Stir the sauce and then pour in wok to heat, stirring continually. When sauce starts to thicken, return all the beef to the wok. Cook until thick and bubbly.

Add the onions and mix to coat everything. Cook for about 1 minute more or until heated through. Serve alone or with rice.

Dad, can you tell me what a solar eclipse is?

No son.

P.F. Chang's Mongolian Beef

This copycat recipe made popular at P.F. Chang's restaurants is a sweeter version of the previous Mongolian Beef recipe in this book. It is well worth the effort and pretty close to the original.

Ingredients:

- 2 teaspoons vegetable oil
- ½ teaspoon ginger, minced
- 1 tablespoon minced garlic
- ½ cup soy sauce
- ½ cup water
- ¾ cup dark brown sugar
- 1 lb flank steak
- ¼ cup cornstarch
- 2 large green onions
- Vegetable oil for frying (about 1 cup)

Directions:

To make the sauce, heat 2 teaspoons of vegetable oil in a medium saucepan over medium heat. Do not let it get too hot. Add the ginger and garlic to the pan and stir. Add the soy sauce and water before the garlic scorches. Add the brown sugar to the sauce and allow the sauce to come to a boil. Let boil for 2 to 3 minutes until the sauce thickens, stirring constantly. Remove from heat and set aside. Bias slice the green onions bias into 1 inch pieces and set aside.

Slice the flank steak against the grain into ¼ inch thick bite sized pieces. Tilt the knife blade at about a 45-degree angle to the top of the steak to provide wider cuts.

Dip the steak pieces in the cornstarch to allow a very thin layer of cornstarch to coat both sides of each piece of steak. Let the steak sit for about 10 minutes to allow the cornstarch to stick to the steak.

Heat up the 1-cup of oil in a wok or deep skillet (deep enough to allow the steak to be covered) over medium/medium-high heat until the oil is hot, but not smoking. Add the steak to the oil, in batches if necessary, and sauté for just two minutes, stirring around so that it cooks evenly. The steak doesn't need to be thoroughly cooked since it will be going bake later for further cooking. Remove the meat using a slotted spoon or tangs onto paper towels. Remove the oil from the wok or skillet.

Put the pan back over the heat and add the meat back and let it simmer for about a minute. Add the sauce and cook for one minute while stirring to coat all the meat, and then add the green onions. Cook for one more minute then, using a slotted spoon or tongs, remove the beef and onions to a serving plate leaving the excess sauce behind in the pan. You may sprinkle the meat with sesame seeds if desired.

P.F. Chang's Mongolian Beef

Her: "I don't even know what the cloning machine does?"

Me: "Well, that makes two of us."

Pepper Steak

This recipe is so much better than normal restaurant fare. Keep the peppers crisp. There is nothing worse than pepper steak with soggy peppers! Real people love pepper steak. This is another family favorite.

Ingredients:

- 1 flank steak (about 1½ pounds.)
- 2 good size green peppers
- 2 tablespoons of rice wine or cooking sherry (pale dry is best)
- 4 tablespoons of soy sauce
- 1 tablespoon of cornstarch
- 2 teaspoons of sugar
- Fresh ginger root (powdered ginger is ok)
- Peanut oil
- Two cups of cooked rice
-

Directions:

In a medium sized mixing bowl, mix the wine, soy sauce, sugar and cornstarch.

Next cut the flank steak across the grain into slices approximately 1½ inches long by ½ inch wide in size. It is easiest to cut the steak when it is partially frozen. Cut against the grain of the meat; this makes the meat tenderer. As you cut them, add the meat to the soy mixture and mix to coat all the pieces. Refrigerate for one to two hours, or as much as 6 hours, mixing occasionally.

Wash and clean the peppers and cut them into 1 to 1½-inch pieces. Place in a bowl and put aside until cooking time.

Start to cook the rice before you start the pepper steak so that the two will be done at the same time. Take out the cut steak. Mix one last time and then drain off the extra liquid.

Put a tablespoon of peanut oil in the wok and swish around to coat the entire inside. Turn the heat up to high until the oil starts to smoke. Add the peppers; turn down the heat to medium high and cook, stirring constantly, for about 3 or 4 minutes. Remove and place aside in a large bowl or platter.

Turn the heat back up to high. Add a tablespoon of oil and a couple of thin slices of the ginger root. Add a small portion of meat and stir fry until cooked, usually about 1 minute. Remove the meat and place with the peppers. (If you are using powdered ginger, add about ¼ teaspoon to the wok with a little oil for each new batch of meat.) Remove the ginger when they start to burn and put in new slices. Continue the above until all the meat is cooked. When the last batch is done, add all the cooked meat and peppers back into the wok and cook and stir for another 1 to 2 minutes shutting off the heat about half way through. Serve immediately over a bed of the cooked rice. Serves 4 to 6 depending on the appetites of the crowd!

Pepper Steak

In ancient Rome, deli workers were told that they could eat anything they wanted during the lunch hour. Anything, that is except the smoked salmon.
Thus were created the world's first anti-lox breaks.

Hibachi Steak

Since most people do not have an Hibachi grill at our disposal, this tasty dish uses two separate skillets to produce the different flavors before combining for the final product.

Ingredients:

- 2 tablespoons canola oil
- 1 large carrot, thinly sliced
- 1 zucchini, thinly sliced
- 1 medium onion, thinly sliced
- 1 8-ounce package of sliced mushrooms
- 1 ½ pounds top round steak (or whatever cut you prefer)
- ½ pound wide fettuccine
- ½ cup reduced sodium soy sauce
- 2 tablespoons cider vinegar
- 2 teaspoons chopped garlic
- 1 teaspoon cornstarch
- 2 tablespoons butter

Directions:

In a small bowl combine the soy sauce, vinegar, garlic, and cornstarch and set aside.

Bring a large pot of salted water to a boil over medium heat. Cook the fettuccine according to directions. Drain and add to a serving bowl or platter.

While the fettuccine is cooking, place a large skillet or wok over medium-high heat and add half of the oil. When the oil is hot, add the vegetables and stir-fry until the vegetables are almost done, about 5 minutes. When the vegetables are done, remove them to a platted and keep warm.

Clean out the skillet and add the remaining oil. Cut the steak into small cubes, and stir-fry until browned on all sides, about 4 to 5 minutes.

Add the vegetables to the steak, along with any accumulated juices, to the skillet. Stir the cornstarch mixture and add it to the skillet and cook until the sauce has thickened, about 2 to 3 minutes. Stir in the butter until melted.

Top the cooked fettuccine with the steak and vegetable mixture and serve.

Hibachi Steak

Patient: Nurse, I keep seeing spots in front of my eyes.

Nurse: Have you seen a doctor?

Patient: No, just spots.

Spice-Rubbed Flank Steak

Flank steak is one of my favorite cuts of beef. It is just so versatile and can be used in many types of recipes, as can be seen in this cookbook. But this recipe is as simple as they come and the result is a tasty tender steak that goes with just about anything.

Ingredients:

- 1 - 1 ½ pound flank steak
- 1 tablespoon of brown sugar
- 1 teaspoon of ground cumin
- ½ teaspoon of salt
- ½ teaspoon of garlic powder
- ½ teaspoon of dried thyme
- ½ teaspoon of cinnamon
- ½ teaspoon of cayenne (or to taste)

Directions:

Mix all the ingredients except the steak in a small bowl; rub mixture over all sides of the steak.

Broil under high heat 6 minutes per side or until cooked.

Remove the steak and let stand for about 3 to 5 minutes; then cut thin slices diagonally against the grain and serve.

Serves 3 to 4.

I went to the butcher's the other day to bet him 50 bucks that he couldn't reach the meat off the top shelf. He said, "No, the steaks are too high."

Grilled Flank Steak With Onions

Here is another simple and very tasty recipe for flank steak.

Ingredients:

- 1 ¼ - 1 ½ pound flank steak
- 2 medium onions (more if desired), cut into rings
- ¼ cup of balsamic vinegar
- 2 teaspoons of Dijon mustard
- 1 teaspoon salt
- 1 teaspoon of chopped fresh rosemary
- 1 tablespoon sea salt
- ½ teaspoon black pepper
- ½ teaspoon allspice
- 1 tablespoon olive oil

Directions:

Mix the vinegar, mustard, salt, black pepper, allspice, rosemary and olive oil in a large shallow glass dish. Add the steak and onions; let marinade for about 20 minutes turning several times to coat.

Grill the steak either on a grill or skillet 7 minutes on each side. You can grill the onions with the steak or separately. Use the remaining marinade to baste the steak and onions during cooking.

Cut the steak across the grain and serve with the onions.

Serves 3 to 4.

Grilled Flank Steak with Onions

I sometimes like my steak undercooked...

But that's rare.

Stir-Fried Beef Tenderloin with Vegetables

This is one of the best, tastiest, mouth-watering Oriental beef dishes you will ever have. Nothing beats a good cut of beef, and tenderloin is the best.

Ingredients:

- 1 pound beef tenderloin
- 4 large mushrooms – about 2 inch in diameter
- ¼ cup fresh snow peas
- 1 teaspoon sugar
- 2 tablespoons soy sauce
- 1 tablespoon Chinese rice wine or pale dry sherry
- 2 teaspoons cornstarch
- 6 peeled fresh water chestnuts sliced ¼ inch thick
- 3 tablespoons peanut oil
- 4 slices fresh ginger root about 1 inch x 1/8 inch
- ½ teaspoon salt

Directions:

Cut the mushrooms into quarters.

Trim off the tips of the snow peas. Blanch the pea pods by dropping them into boiling water. They will turn bright green in less than 1 minute. Immediately drain and run under cold water to stop the cooking and preserve the color. Set aside.

Trim away any fat on the tenderloin and cut into one-inch cubes or 1½ to 2-inch strips.

In a bowl, combine the sugar, soy sauce, wine and cornstarch. Mix them together thoroughly. Add the beef cubes and mix in the bowl until all the meat is coated.

Have all of the above, plus the oil, ginger and salt within easy reach.

Set a wok or 10-inch skillet over high heat for about 30 seconds. Add 1 tablespoon of oil and swirl around to coat the pan for another 30 seconds or until the oil begins to smoke. Turn down the heat to medium high. Add the mushrooms, snow peas and water chestnuts and stir-fry for about two minutes making sure they are totally coated with the oil. Add the salt and stir for a few moments and then remove the vegetables to a plate.

Pour in the remaining 2 tablespoons of oil into the pan. Add the ginger and turn the heat to high. Drop in the beef and stir-fry for 2 to 3 minutes until the meat is lightly browned on all sides. Pick out and discard the ginger. Add the vegetables in with the meat and stir-fry long enough to heat the vegetables through. Plate the entire contents and serve immediately.

Serves 2 to 4.

Luke and Obi-Wan are in a Chinese restaurant having a meal. Skillfully using his chopsticks, Obi-Wan deftly dishes himself a large portion of noodles into his bowl, then tops it off with some chicken and cashew nuts. All this is done with consummate ease you'd expect from a Jedi Master.

Poor old Luke is having a nightmare, using his chopsticks in both hands, dropping his food all over the table and eventually himself.

Obi-Wan looks at Luke disapprovingly and says, "Use the FORKS, Luke."

Steak Diane

This is an easy "showy" dish that was originally created to be cooked at tableside in fancy restaurants. Flaming dishes are always fun. Watch your eyebrows!

Ingredients:

- 1 to ½ lbs sirloin steak cut ½ inch thick (rump steak will work, too) in two pieces
- ¾ cup mushrooms, sliced
- 2 cloves garlic finely chopped
- 1 onion, chopped
- 3 tablespoons butter
- 1 tablespoon Worcestershire Sauce
- 4-5 tablespoons Brandy
- Salt and pepper to taste
- Chopped parsley for garnish

Directions::

Flatten the steak slightly by pounding with a flat pan or meat mallet making sure not to damage the meat.

Heat ½ of the butter in a large frying pan and cook the onion, garlic and mushrooms for about 3 minutes over medium-high heat. Push the vegetables out to the side of the pan where they can continue to cook more slowly.

Add the rest of the butter and add the steaks and cook to the desired doneness, about 2 minutes per side should do medium-rare. Add the salt and pepper, Worcestershire Sauce, parsley and then the Brandy. Once the Brandy has warmed, carefully ignite it and serve at once.

Serves 2

A group of nuns are touring the White House in Washington D.C. As the tour ends, they are waiting in line to sign the visitors' registry, followed by a Jewish family with their young son Sheldon. As they near the registry, young Sheldon loses patience and runs ahead to sign the book. However, his mother stops him and admonishes him saying, "Wait till the nun signs Shelly!"

Italian Style Veal Cutlets

Everyone that I know loves good old-fashioned Italian breaded veal cutlets. This is the standard recipe for breading almost anything, veal, chicken, fish, eggplant and even chicken fried steak.

Ingredients:

- 4 large pounded veal cutlets*
- 2 cups Italian bread crumbs
- 2 eggs, beaten
- 1 cup flour
- ½ cup Olive oil
- Salt and pepper to taste

Directions:

Place the flour and breadcrumbs in two separate deep dishes. Place the eggs in a 3rd deep dish or wide bowl. In turn, take each cutlet and dredge it in the flour making sure that the entire cutlet is covered. Shake off the excess. Next, dredge the cutlet in the eggs and let the excess drip off back into the bowl. Place the cutlet in the bowl with the breadcrumbs, making sure to cover every part of the cutlet. Press the cutlet into the crumbs and/or cover with crumbs and press lightly into the cutlet. Shake off excess and place the breaded cutlet on a clean plate. Repeat for all the cutlets.

Pour the olive oil into a large skillet and heat over med heat. When the oil is very hot, place as many cutlets as can fit in the skillet leaving about ½ inch between each. Cook over moderate heat until the bottoms of the cutlets are a deep golden brown, about 4-5 minutes. Turn over the cutlets and cook the other side. Remove and place on a rack or paper towel to allow the oil to drain. Place them in a 250° F oven until ready to serve. Serve with fresh lemon.

*You can buy veal cutlets already pounded, but if not, it is simple to do. Take an 18-inch sheet of waxed paper and place it on a sturdy counter top. Place one cutlet in the center of one half of the paper and fold the other half over to cover the cutlet. With a pounding mallet, or a small heavy skillet with a flat bottom, evenly pound the cutlet until it is about half its original thickness. Make sure you pound with the flat part of whatever you use to pound with as corners will tear the waxed paper and damage the meat. Repeat for all the cutlets. If using eggplant, do not pound!

"My favorite animal is steak."
- Fran Lebowitz

Chicken or Veal Parmesan

An essential part of any Italian restaurant menu and one of my favorite dishes.

Ingredients:

- 4 veal cutlets, 4-6 ounces each, or 4 chicken breast halves
- My Spaghetti Gravy (see recipe)
- 8 ounces sliced or shredded Mozzarella cheese, fresh Mozzarella is the best
- Grated Parmesan cheese

Directions:

Use the recipe for Italian Veal cutlets to prepare the veal or chicken.

Place cutlets in baking dish coated with My Spaghetti Gravy. Liberally spoon the gravy over the cutlets. Liberally place sliced or shredded Mozzarella cheese over cutlets to the desired thickness. Bake in a 350° F oven for 10 to 15 minutes. Top with Parmesan cheese and serve with spaghetti and a tossed salad.

Chicken Parmesan

Veal and Shallots

Veal is one of my favorite meats, so I had to include several veal recipes in this book. This is a simple and very tasty veal dish. The shallots and the sauce really enhance the veal.

Ingredients:

- 2 large veal cutlets, pounded thin
- 1 large shallot, sliced thin
- 2 tablespoons olive oil
- 1 tablespoon butter
- ½ cup Madeira wine
- ¼ cup chicken stock
- 2 garlic cloves, minced
- Salt and pepper

Directions:

In a large skillet over medium heat, melt the butter and add the olive oil. While this is heating, salt and pepper both sides of the cutlets. Place the veal in the skillet and cook until each piece starts to brown slightly, about 2 minutes. Turn the veal over and cook the same on the other side. Remove the veal to a heated plate.

Add the shallots and garlic to the pan and stir-fry just until the shallots start to wilt. Add the wine and stir-fry until the wine is reduced by half. Add the stock and continue to cook until the liquid is reduced and thickens slightly.

Pour the sauce and shallots over each piece of veal and serve immediately.

Serves 2. This dish is especially good with fresh asparagus.

"I went on a diet, swore off drinking and heavy eating, and in fourteen days
I had lost exactly two weeks." – Joe E. Lewis

Veal Marsala

Sometimes I think that Marsala wine was made just to make this recipe, although I do use it in a lot of cooking. You could also make Chicken Marsala using the same recipe.

Ingredients:

- 4 veal cutlets (about 3-4 ounces each)
- Salt and freshly ground black pepper
- 2 tablespoons unsalted butter
- 3 tablespoons olive oil
- 2 shallot, chopped
- 2 teaspoons chopped garlic
- 4 ounces fresh mushrooms, sliced
- 1 cup Marsala wine
- 1 cup veal or chicken stock
- ¼ cup fresh chopped parsley leaves

Directions:

Sprinkle the veal with salt and pepper. Melt 1 tablespoon of butter and 1 tablespoon of oil in a large, heavy skillet over medium-high heat. Add the 4 veal cutlets and cook until golden brown, about 2 minutes per side. Transfer the veal to a plate.

Add 2 tablespoons of oil to the skillet. Add the shallot and garlic. Sauté until fragrant, about 30 seconds. Add the mushrooms and season with salt. Add the Marsala and simmer until the Marsala reduces by half. Add the veal stock and parsley. Simmer 1 more minute. Return the veal to the skillet. Stir the remaining tablespoon of butter into the sauce. Season the sauce with salt and pepper, to taste. Serve with buttered egg noodles or rice.

Veal Marsala

What is that sound?" a woman asked at our nature center.

"It's the frogs trilling for a mate," Patti, the naturalist, explained. "We have a pair in the science room. But since they've been together for so long, they no longer sing to each other."

The woman nodded sympathetically, "Ah, the trill is gone."

Wiener Schnitzel

Schnitzel is a traditional Austrian dish of either breaded veal (traditional) or pork. Included here are the three secrets for making the perfect Schnitzel.

Ingredients:

- 4 veal cutlets pounded to ¼ inch thickness (pork may be used instead of veal)
- ¼ cup flour
- ½ teaspoon salt
- ½ cup plain breadcrumbs
- 2 tablespoons parsley flakes (optional)
- 2 eggs
- Oil for frying (lard is traditional)

Directions:

Place the breadcrumbs in a food processor and pulse them until they are no longer coarse, but not as fine as flour. This is secret number one.

Set up 3 shallow dishes. Place the flour and ½ teaspoon salt in one and breadcrumbs mixed with parsley in another. Beat the eggs well and place in the third dish.

Heat at least ¼ inch of oil in the pan to 350°F. Make sure the breaded meat "swims" in oil/fat. Contrary to instinct, the breading will take on less oil this way than if the meat is sticking to the pan. This is secret number two.

Working one at a time, dredge cutlets first in flour until the surface is completely dry. Dip in egg to coat, allow the excess to drip off for a few seconds and then roll quickly in the breadcrumbs until coated. Do not press breadcrumbs into the meat. The crust should not adhere completely, but form a loose shell around the schnitzel. This is secret number three.

Place the meat immediately in the pan with the hot oil (do not let the cutlet sit in a dish while you prepare more). Do not crowd the pan. Cook the schnitzel in batches, if necessary.

Fry the schnitzel for 3-4 minutes on one side. You may want to move them around a little with your fork to make sure they are not sticking to the pan. Turn them over once and fry until both sides are golden brown. Do not over cook. Remove from pan, allow the oil to drain off, place on a plate with lemon slices, or serve with Spaetzle and Jaeger Schnitzel Sauce (see recipes).

Serves 4.

Wiener Schnitzel with Spaetzle and Jaeger Schnitzel Sauce

A dog gave birth to puppies near the side of the road and was cited for littering.

Lemon Chicken

This is an easy lemon-chicken recipe that is a very popular main dish. Just add fresh crisp veggies and some rice for sides. This is just one of the countless variations on this dish.

Ingredients:
- 1 lb. boneless, skinless chicken breast
- 6 tablespoons corn starch
- 2 tablespoons flour
- 1 sliced lemon, for garnish
- 1 teaspoon Sesame oil
- ½ cup chicken stock

Lemon Sauce:
- 1/4 cup chicken stock
- 1 teaspoon sesame oil (optional)
- 1/4 cup sugar
- 1/2 teaspoon salt
- 2 teaspoons corn starch
- Juice of 1 lemon (about 1/4 cup)

Marinade:
- 1/2 teaspoon salt
- 2 teaspoons rice wine or dry sherry
- 1 teaspoon soy sauce
- 1/8 teaspoon pepper

Directions:

Cut the chicken breasts into thin slices. Combine the marinade ingredients in a medium-sized bowl. Add the chicken. Mix well. Let stand for 30 minutes.

Combine the ingredients for the lemon sauce in a small bowl. Mix well and set aside.

Meanwhile, mix the 6 tablespoons of cornstarch and the 2 tablespoons of flour in a medium-sized bowl. Dip the chicken pieces in the flour mixture to coat.

Heat the ¼ cup of chicken stock in a fry pan and brown the chicken in the stock. Continue adding more additional stock as needed to prevent burning. Remove the chicken, arrange on a platter.

Stir the lemon sauce into the hot pan. Bring to a boil. When the sauce begins to thicken, add 1 teaspoon of the sesame oil. Stir the sauce and pour over the chicken. If desired, garnish with the lemon slices. Serve immediately.

Chicken Marengo

This is one of the earliest "fancy" dishes I loved to make. It is very simple yet good enough for company. This famous dish of braised chicken with onions and mushrooms in a wine and tomato sauce (that name was too long so they shortened it) is named after Napoleon's victory at the Battle of Marengo on June 14, 1800. According to tradition, Napoleon demanded a quick meal after the battle and his chef was forced to work with the meager results of forage. Local lore says it was cooked on the battlefield (another word for kitchen, I think).

Ingredients:

- One 2 pound roasting chicken, jointed or 4 chicken quarters*
- ¼ cup olive oil
- 1 small onion, chopped
- 1 or 2 garlic cloves, crushed or minced
- 3 tablespoons flour
- ½ cup medium dry white wine
- 1 cup chicken stock
- 1 tablespoon tomato paste
- 1 – 1½ cups of small button mushrooms or larger ones halved or quartered
- Fresh parsley, chopped
- Salt and pepper

Directions:

Lightly salt and pepper the chicken pieces. Heat the oil in a large heatproof casserole and fry the chicken parts over moderate heat until golden brown all over. Add the onion and garlic and cook with the chicken. Add the flour and cook for a minute (I find it easier to stack the chicken at this step and cook the flour with the chicken drippings, onion and garlic by themselves). Add the wine, stock and tomato paste and stir to combine. The liquid should just cover the chicken. Salt and pepper to taste. Add the mushrooms and mix well with the chicken. Cover and let gently simmer for about 40 minutes.

Place the chicken on a serving dish and reduce the sauce if necessary and pour over the chicken. Garnish with chopped parsley. Can be served over rice if desired.

Instead of chicken joints, which are traditional, you may use boneless chicken breasts and/or thighs so you will not have to contend with bones.

Chicken Marengo

A woman was working in her yard with the weed whacker, when she accidentally cut off the tail of her cat.

She ran screaming into the house, and told her husband, wondering what to do.

He replied calmly, "Get the cat, and the tail, and we'll take them to Wal-Mart."

She was incredulous. "How could that possibly help?" she asked.

"Well," he replied, "they're the world's largest retailer."

Chicken Pot Pie

I grew up eating those frozen chicken and turkey pot pies. I must confess that I liked them. But home made is so much better because you control all that goes into the pie as well as how much goes in each one.

Ingredients:

- 1 large chicken breast
- 1 large potato
- 2 medium carrots
- 1 medium onion, chopped or frozen pearl onions, blanched
- 3 stalks celery
- ½ cup frozen peas
- ¼ cup of fresh parsley, chopped
- 2 cups chicken stock
- ¼ cup dry white wine (optional)
- ¼ cup flour
- 5 tablespoons unsalted butter
- Salt and pepper to taste
- Frozen readymade puff pastry or pie crust
- Parmesan cheese

Directions:

Preheat the oven to 350° F.

Take two sheets of puff pastry or piecrust, out of the freezer to thaw. Dice the potato, your choice skin on or off, in a large dice. Cut the carrots and celery into ½ inch pieces and add the onion. Place all the vegetables in a bowl and set aside.

Cut the chicken into bite sized pieces. Heat a large skillet over medium-high heat and when hot add the chicken and stir-fry until the chicken is cooked on all sides, but not browned. Remove the chicken and set aside.

In the same skillet add 1 tablespoon of butter. When melted, add the vegetables and stir-fry them until just tender. Remove the vegetables and set aside.

Lower the heat to medium and add the remaining butter. When melted, add the flour and whisk until smooth to make a roux. Continue cooking and whisking for about 2 minutes to cook out the flour taste. Add the chicken stock and whisk until the sauce becomes thick and smooth.

Stir in the wine, and add salt and pepper to taste. Add the vegetables to the sauce and mix well until the vegetables are reheated. Add the chicken and any accumulated juices and mix well. Add the frozen peas, the parsley and then mix. Taste and season as desired. Continue to cook for a few minutes and remove from the stove.

Individual Chicken Pot Pies

Lay the thawed pastry sheets on a lightly floured cool surface. Invert individual crocks being used, or a shallow casserole, on the pastry sheet and, using a sharp knife, cut circles around the outside of the bowls, slightly larger than the bowl itself. Spray the inside of each crock or casserole with non-stick vegetable spray. Fill each of the crocks or casserole ¾ of the way with the chicken mixture. Do not fill too high because the contents will overflow the sides while cooking. Cap each crock or the casserole with a pastry circle, pressing the dough around the rim to form a seal. Cut two or three slits in the top of the dough to allow steam to escape. Lightly beat the egg with 3 tablespoons of water to make an egg wash and brush some on the pastry. Sprinkle the pastry with the Parmesan cheese. Set the containers on a cookie sheet and transfer to the oven. Bake for 20 minutes or until puffed and golden.

Serves 4 to 6.

What do you call an Egyptian back specialist?

A Cairo-practor!

Teriyaki Chicken Meatballs (Tsukune)

Teriyaki chicken *tsukune* (meatballs in Japanese) are a favorite dish in Japan and are also a favorite among kids. These tasty meatballs can be used as part of a main dinner course for dinner, or the recipe can easily be doubled and used as an appetizer or even dressed-up on individual bamboo toothpicks as an hors d'oeuvre. Try using ground turkey instead of chicken.

Ingredients:

- **For the meatballs (tsukune)**
- 1 pound ground chicken breast
- ½ onion, finely chopped
- 1 piece grated ginger (or 1 teaspoon pre-grated ginger in tube)
- 1 ½ tablespoons sake
- 1 ½ tablespoons soy sauce
- 1 teaspoon cornstarch
- 1 egg
- 1/3 cup Panko bread crumbs
- 1 to 2 teaspoons canola oil
-
- **For the teriyaki sauce**
- 2 tablespoons granulated sugar
- ¼ cup soy sauce
- ½ cup mirin
- ½ cup sake
- Roasted sesame seeds as garnish, optional
- Finely sliced scallions as garnish (optional)

Direction:

In a medium bowl combine ingredients for the teriyaki sauce: granulated sugar, soy sauce, mirin, and sake. Mix until the sugar is all dissolved and set aside.

In a large bowl add the onion, ground chicken breast, grated ginger, sake, soy sauce, cornstarch, egg, and breadcrumbs. Knead with hands to incorporate all ingredients. Note, the mixture will be very soft but will hold together.

Line a large plate with plastic wrap or waxed paper. Begin making small meatballs, about 2 teaspoons in size, and arrange them on the lined plate to prepare them for cooking.

In a large frying pan, heat oil on medium heat, making sure the oil coats the pan. Place meatballs in the pan, making sure not to overcrowd the pan or allow the meatballs to touch each other. Cook meatballs for about 4 minutes on each side until browned and they hold together. Note, because the meatball mixture is so soft, I recommend using a slotted spoon and spatula together to help flip the meatballs over. The meatballs do not need to be completely cooked through as these will be cooked again with the sauce later. Once the meatballs are browned on both sides, remove from the pan onto a clean plate and set aside. This may need to be done twice to accommodate all the meatballs.

Using the same frying pan, add the teriyaki sauce ingredients and cook on medium-high heat, while gently scraping the bits and pieces off the bottom of the pan. Continue to cook the sauce, about 2 to 3 minutes until it bubbles. Slightly lower the heat to medium-low.

Add the cooked meatballs back into the pan and gently roll in the teriyaki sauce. Continue to cook the meatballs in the teriyaki sauce until the sauce begins to reduce and slightly thickens.

Plate the meatballs, pouring excess sauce over them. If desired, garnish with roasted sesame seeds or finely sliced green scallions.

Teriyaki Chicken Meatballs (Tsukune)

What's the definition of a will? (It's a dead giveaway).

Aloha Chicken

This is an easy and tasty recipe to jazz up the normal everyday chicken recipes.

Ingredients:

- 4 boneless, skinless chicken breast halves
- 1 tablespoon flour
- 1 tablespoon oil
- 16 ounce can of pineapple chunks
- 1 teaspoon cornstarch
- ¼ cup chicken stock or water
- 1 tablespoon honey
- 1 tablespoon teriyaki sauce or soy sauce
- 1/8 teaspoon pepper

Directions:

Pound the chicken breasts to ¼ inch thickness. If desired, the chicken can be cut into large bite sized pieces or leave as cutlets. Place the flour in a large zip-lock plastic bag. Add the chicken and shake to coat.

Heat the oil in a large skillet over medium heat. Brown the chicken in oil until the juices run clear. Remove the chicken from the skillet and keep warm then add the stock to the skillet.

Drain the pineapple, reserving ¼ cup of juice; drink the rest. In a small bowl, combine the pineapple juice and cornstarch until smooth; add to the skillet with the stock. Stir in the honey, teriyaki sauce and the pepper. Bring to a slow boil until sauce thickens. Add the pineapple and chicken and stir to evenly coat everything. Heat thoroughly. Serve on a bed of rice. Serves 4.

"If a mute swears, does his mother wash his hands with soap?"
-George Carlin

Roasted Herbed Chicken

This recipe is for those who really like to get into their food… literally. Putting the herbs between the skin and the meat intensifies the herb flavoring in the meat substantially. It's actually a lot of fun, too. Good therapy.

Ingredients:

- 3 tablespoons extra-virgin olive oil
- 2 cloves garlic chopped.
- 1 tablespoon Garlic salt
- 1 tablespoon Onion powder
- 1 teaspoon Fresh Ground Pepper
- 2 tablespoons Basil
- 1 tablespoon Thyme
- 1 cup white wine, any kind that you like to drink is best
- 1 whole chicken split and cleaned
- Fresh parsley, fine cut.
- ½ cup chicken stock
- 1 tablespoon corn starch dissolved in 2 tablespoons of water

Directions:

In a small bowl, mix the Garlic salt, Onion powder, pepper, basil, and thyme.

Place the two chicken halves on a baking sheet skin side up. Using your fingers, gently lift the skin on the chicken to make pockets under the breast and leg skin. If the skin doesn't come up freely, a very sharp knife, such as a fillet knife, can be used to detach the skin from the meat to form a pocket. Liberally spread the herb and spice mixture on the meat under the skin. Pull the skin back to its original position to trap the seasoning between the meat and the skin. Use the remaining mixture to sprinkle over the top and bottom outsides of the chicken. Let stand for at least ½ hour to an hour skin side up.

Preheat the oven to 375° F.

In a large cast iron skillet, or other oven capable skillet, heat the oil under medium-high heat. Add the garlic and cook for about 1 minute, stirring so not to burn. Place the chicken onto the skillet, skin side down. Cook the chicken until the skin is brown, not burned. Add ½ the wine and shut off the heat. Turn the chicken over, now skin side up, and place skillet in the oven and cook for 35 minutes.

Remove the skillet from the oven and place back on the stove. Plate the chicken. Pour off any oil and fat from the top of the juices in the skillet. Turn the stove to medium; add the chicken stock and the rest of the wine to the skillet. Stir, scraping the cooked parts from the bottom of the skillet. Reduce the liquid to about half. Add the cornstarch, a small amount at a time, to thicken. Pour over the chicken and any desired vegetables. Garnish with parsley. Serve immediately.

A group of chess enthusiasts checked into a hotel and were standing in the lobby discussing their recent tournament victories. After about an hour, the manager came out of the office and asked them to disperse .

"But why?" they asked, as they moved off.

"Because," he said, "I can't stand chess-nuts boasting in an open foyer."

Chicken, Sausage and Peppers

This is an easy and very tasty dish that brings out a great flavor combination of chicken and sausage. This is another one of those "break the monotony" recipes.

Ingredients:

- 2 tablespoons unsalted butter
- ¾ pound sweet or hot Italian sausage
- ¾ pound skinless, boneless chicken breasts
- Kosher salt and freshly ground pepper
- 1 tablespoon all-purpose flour
- 1 small onion, chopped
- 2 Italian green frying peppers, cut into 1-inch pieces
- 3 cloves garlic, roughly chopped
- ½ cup dry white wine
- ¾ cup low-sodium chicken broth
- ¼ cup roughly chopped fresh parsley
- 2 jarred pickled cherry peppers, chopped, plus 2 tablespoons liquid from the jar

Directions:

Cut the sausage into chunks or ½ inch slices. It is best if the sausage is partially frozen when sliced. Cut the chicken into bite sized slices and place in a separate bowl.

Heat 1 tablespoon of butter in a large skillet over medium-high heat. Cook the sausage until golden, about 2 minutes. Season the chicken with salt and pepper, then toss with the flour in a bowl; add to the skillet with the sausage and cook until browned but not cooked through, about 3 minutes. Add the onion, peppers, garlic, ½ teaspoon salt, and pepper to taste and cook 3 minutes. Add the wine, scraping up any browned bits on the bottom of the skillets; bring to a boil and cook until slightly reduced, about 1 minute. Add the broth and bring to a gentle simmer. Cover and cook until the sausage and chicken are cooked through, about 5 minutes.

Transfer the chicken, sausage and vegetables to a platter with a slotted spoon. Increase the heat to high and stir the parsley and cherry peppers and their liquid into the skillet; boil until the liquid is reduced by one-third, 2 to 3 minutes. Remove from the heat and stir in the remaining tablespoon butter. Pour the sauce over the chicken mixture and serve. Serves 4.

What did Noah say as he was loading the Ark? "Now I herd everything"

Chicken and Asparagus Stir-Fry

This is a great and easy dinner that consists of just 2 main ingredients, 3 if you count the rice.

Ingredients:

- 1 pound boneless skinless chicken breasts
- 3 cloves garlic, minced
- 1 teaspoon ground ginger
- 1 tablespoon soy sauce
- 1 tablespoon sugar
- 1 tablespoon plus 1 teaspoon cornstarch
- ½ teaspoons kosher salt
- 1 tablespoon dry sherry
- ¾ cup chicken broth or water
- 2 tablespoons vegetable oil
- 2 pounds fresh asparagus (1 or 2 bunches depending on thickness)
- 1 bunch scallions (white and green parts), thinly sliced
- 2 cups rice (cooked)

Directions:

Wash and trim the asparagus (I use the snapping method and it has always worked perfectly for me) and discard the woody stems. Slice into 1-½ inch pieces and set aside.

In a medium mixing bowl add half the garlic and ginger, the soy sauce, sugar, 1 teaspoon of the cornstarch, 1 teaspoon of salt, and the sherry; mix well. Slice the chicken against the grain into thin 1-½ inch strips and add to the marinade. Marinate at room temperature for about 20 minutes, stirring occasionally. Mix the remaining cornstarch with ½ cup of the broth.

Heat 1 tablespoon of the oil a large nonstick skillet over high heat. Add the asparagus, scallions, remaining garlic, ginger, ¼ cup of broth, and season with the teaspoon salt. Stir-fry until the asparagus is bright green but still crisp, about 3 minutes. Transfer to a bowl.

Heat the same skillet until very hot and then add remaining 1 tablespoon of oil. Add the chicken and marinade and stir-fry until the edges start to turn brown, about 3 minutes. Reduce the heat to medium; return the asparagus to the pan and toss to heat through. Stir in the reserved cornstarch mixture and cook until thickened. Serve over a bed of rice.

Chicken and Asparagus Stir-Fry

Did you hear about the magic tractor?
It was driving down the road and suddenly turned into a field.

Italian Baked Chicken and Pasta

Here is a different chicken dish to break up the monotony of the same old chicken.

Ingredients:

- 1 cup pastina pasta (or any small pasta)
- 2 tablespoons olive oil
- ½ cup cubed chicken breast (1-inch cubes)
- ½ cup diced onion (about ½ a small onion)
- 1 clove garlic, minced
- 1 (14.5-ounce) can diced tomatoes with juice
- 1 cup shredded mozzarella
- ¼ cup chopped fresh flat-leaf parsley
- ¼ teaspoon kosher salt
- ¼ teaspoon freshly ground black pepper
- ¼ cup bread crumbs
- ¼ cup grated Parmesan
- 1 tablespoon butter, plus more for buttering the baking dish

Directions:

Preheat the oven to 400° F.

Bring a medium pot of salted water to a boil over high heat. Add the pasta and cook until just al dente, stirring occasionally, about 5 minutes. Drain pasta and put into a large mixing bowl.

Meanwhile, put the olive oil in a medium sauté pan over medium heat. Add the chicken and cook for 3 minutes. Add the onions and garlic, stirring to combine, and cook until the onions are soft and the chicken is cooked through, about 5 minutes more.

Put the chicken mixture into the bowl with the cooked pasta. Add the canned tomatoes, mozzarella cheese, parsley, salt, and pepper. Stir to combine. Place the mixture in a buttered 8 by 8 by 2-inch baking dish. In a small bowl mix together the breadcrumbs and the Parmesan cheese. Sprinkle over the top of the pasta mixture. Dot the top with small bits of butter. Bake until the top is golden brown, about 30 minutes. Serves 4.

Italian Baked Chicken and Pasta

"The trouble with eating Italian food is that five or six days later you're hungry again."
- George Miller.

Stir-Fried Hoisin Chicken

Here is yet another Chinese dish that is, like most stir-fry recipes, easy to make.

Ingredients:

- 1 boneless skinless full chicken breast or 6-8 large chicken tenders cut into ½ inch cubes/strips
- 1 tablespoon of cornstarch
- 2 tablespoons pale dry sherry
- 1 tablespoon low sodium soy sauce
- 1 large green pepper, seeded and cut into ½ inch squares
- 1 8-ounce can of water chestnuts cut into ¼ inch pieces
- 6 ounces fresh mushrooms cut into 1 inch by ½ inch slices
- ½ teaspoon of Kosher salt
- 2 tablespoons Hoisin sauce
- 3 tablespoons peanut oil for frying
- Optional: ¼ cup cashews, peanuts or almonds

Directions:

Add the chicken to a large bowl and sprinkle on the cornstarch and mix until the chicken is totally coated. Add the sherry and soy sauce and again mix until all the chicken is evenly coated.

Place a 12-inch wok or skillet over high heat for about 30 seconds and then add 1 tablespoon of peanut oil. Swirl the oil around to coats the inside of the pan and continue to heat until the oil starts to smoke slightly. Turn down the heat to medium high and add the green peppers, water chestnuts mushrooms and salt. Stir-fry for 2 to 3 minutes then remove all the vegetables to a plate.

Add the remaining oil to the pan and heat under high heat again until the oil starts to smoke. Add the chicken and stir-fry until the chicken turns white and firm, about 3 minutes. Add the Hoisin sauce and continue to stir to coat all the chicken. Add the vegetables back in and continue to stir-fry for another minute. At this point you can add the nuts if they are so desired and stir-fry all for another minute. Serve at once as either a side dish or over rice as a main course.

Serves 2 as a main course and 4 as a side dish.

She criticized my apartment, so I knocked her flat.

Baked Teriyaki Chicken

Tired of "chicken breast this" and "chicken breast that"? This easy little dish uses chicken thighs, which are really tasty with this sauce and are also cheaper than breasts.

Ingredients:

- 8 skinless chicken thighs (boneless are fine to use also)
- 1 tablespoon cornstarch
- 1 tablespoon cold water
- ½ cup brown sugar
- ½ cup soy sauce
- ¼ cups cider vinegar
- 1 clove garlic, minced
- ½ teaspoon ground ginger
- ¼ teaspoon black pepper

Directions:

Preheat the over to 425° F.

Make the teriyaki sauce. Place the cold water, cornstarch, sugar, soy sauce, vinegar, garlic, ginger and black pepper in a small saucepan over low heat. Bring to a simmer and stir frequently until the sauce thickens.

Place the chicken in a lightly greased baking dish and brush each side liberally with the sauce. Put in the oven and bake for 30 minutes, basting with sauce every 10 minutes. Turn the pieces over and repeat for another 30 minutes until the juices from the chicken run clear.

Serve with crisp vegetables and on a bed of rice if desired. There will be a little sauce left which should be poured over the plated chicken or used as a sauce for accompanying vegetables.

Serves 4.

Baked Teriyaki Chicken

Marcy was married to Ed Smith. Unfortunately, she was also married to Ed Jones. The woman was eventually caught, charged with bigamy and brought to trial.

When the incredulous judge asked how she could have done such a thing, Marcy replied, "Well, your honor, you know they say that two Eds are better than one."

Stir-Fried Chicken with Fresh Mushrooms

This is a different combination that is sure to please.

Ingredients:

- 2 whole boneless, skinless chicken breasts cut into bite sized strips
- 4 ounces fresh snow peas, tips removed
- 4 ounces fresh mushrooms, sliced
- 2 teaspoons cornstarch
- 1 egg white
- 1 tablespoon sherry
- 1 teaspoon salt
- 2 slices fresh peeled ginger root
- 4 tablespoons peanut oil
- 1 teaspoon cornstarch dissolved in 1 tablespoon chicken stock or water

Directions:

Combine the chicken and cornstarch in a large mixing bowl and toss until all pieces are evenly coated. Add the egg white, sherry, and ½ teaspoon salt and stir until well mixed.

Heat a 12-inch wok or large skillet over high heat for about 30 seconds. Add 1 tablespoon of oil and swirl around to coat the pan. Lower the heat to medium high when it starts to smoke. Add the mushrooms, snow peas and ½ teaspoon salt and stir-fry for about 2 minutes. Transfer to a platter and set aside.

Add the remaining oil to the pan and let heat about 30 seconds. Add the ginger slices and cook for about 30 seconds, then remove and discard the ginger. Add the chicken and stir-fry until the chicken is firm and white. Return the cooked vegetables and give a quick stir. Give the cornstarch solution a quick stir to recombine it then add it to the pan and cook the contents stirring constantly until all the ingredients are coated with a light clear glaze. Serve at once.

Serves 4.

What do you call a boomerang that doesn't work?

A stick.

Chinese Spare Ribs

Chinese take out made at home. Not quite the same as you get in most restaurants, but I think these are much better and meatier.

Ingredients:

- A 2-pound slab of pork spareribs (the meatier the better)

Marinade:

- ¼ cup soy sauce
- 3 tablespoons honey
- 2 tablespoons Hoisin sauce
- 2 tablespoons white vinegar
- 1 tablespoon Chinese rice wine or pale dry sherry
- 2 teaspoons finely chopped garlic
- 1 teaspoon sugar
- 2 tablespoons chicken stock
- 1 one gallon plastic sealable storage bag (must be air tight)
- A few drops of red food coloring (optional)

Directions:

Trim any excess fat from the ribs. Cut the ribs into sections to a size so that all the sections will fit into the plastic storage bag. Usually 4 or 5 ribs wide will do.

In a small bowl, combine the soy sauce, honey, Hoisin sauce, vinegar, wine, garlic, food coloring, sugar and chicken stock. Stir until all is well mixed and homogeneous. Place the ribs in the plastic bag, put in the marinade and seal the bag forcing out as much air as possible before sealed. Swish the marinade around in the bag so that all the ribs are well coated. Let the ribs marinade for 3 to 4 hours at room temperature, or 6 hours to overnight in the refrigerator, turning the bag over several times during the marinade period.

Cook:

Preheat the oven to 375° F. Place a large roasting pan with about 2 inches of water and place on the lowest rack of the oven. This will catch the drippings from the ribs, stop the oven from smoking and keep the ribs moist while cooking. Insert the curved tips of S-shaped hooks (you can use curtain hooks or lengths of unpainted thick coat hangers bent to shape) into the ribs and hang them from a rack placed in the highest position in the oven over the pan of water, but not touching the water. If hooks are not available, you can use a wire rack over the roasting pan, but the ribs should be cooked on the middle oven rack. Spray the rack with a non-stick spray to easy cleaning.

Roast the ribs for 45 minutes. Then raise the heat to 425° F and cook for 10 minutes longer or until the outside is of the desired crispness.

To serve:

Place the cooked ribs on a chopping board and separate the ribs using a cleaver or heavy-duty knife. Serve hot or cold with plum sweet and sour or other dipping sauce (see recipes).

Chinese Spare Ribs with Plum Sweet and Sour Dipping Sauce and Rice

A city in Alaska passed a law outlawing all dogs.
It became known as Dogless Fairbanks.

Chinatown Char Siu Ribs

This is a low and slow way to do Chinese spare ribs. These cook at a low temperature for a full 3 hours. This way the ribs will not dry out from high heat.

Ingredients:

- 1 slab of Baby Back ribs (about 14 ribs)
- ½ cup of Hoisin Sauce
- ½ cup of brandy (rum or bourbon would also work)
- ¼ cup of honey
- ¼ cup of soy sauce
- 2 tablespoons of toasted sesame Oil
- 2 tablespoons of ginger powder
- 2 tablespoons of onion powder
- 1 tablespoon of garlic powder
- 1 tablespoon of five spice powder
- 1 teaspoon of red food coloring
- 2 tablespoons of hot sauce (your choice) (optional)
- Sesame seeds for garnish

Directions:

Remove the membrane from the bone side of the slab if desired. You can do this by prying a small amount of the membrane back with a knife and then grabbing this bit with a dry paper towel and peel off the membrane. This is not always easy, but it allows the marinade to have more access to the meat.

You may opt to cut the ribs into individual ribs and set aside, or you may cook as an entire slab or anything in between. You may also opt to cut the ribs in half into smaller riblets. You can have your butcher cut the slab in half when you buy them.

To make the marinade, mix all the ingredients except the ribs in a glass bowl. Do not leave out the alcohol. It is used mainly to penetrate the meat while marinating. There is no measurable alcohol in the ribs after cooking. But, if you really don't want to use the alcohol, you may substitute apple juice.

Place the ribs in a seal tight plastic bag and add the marinade. Seal the bag and let the ribs marinate for a minimum of one hour, overnight is better, turning the ribs to coat several times.

Preheat the over to 225° F. Place a rack in a pan with at least ½ inch of water in the bottom. This is to prevent the drippings from burning on the pan. Place the ribs on the rack, bone side down. Cook the ribs for 3 hours. If desired, baste the ribs with honey for the last ½ hour. If you heat the honey first it will be more liquid and easier to baste with. The honey adds a sweetness to the cooked ribs and puts a nice gloss on the final product.

Plate the ribs, garnish with sesame seeds if desired, and serve.

Chinatown Spare Ribs

A guy was telling his friend that he and his wife had a serious argument the night before. "But it ended," he said, "when she came crawling to me on her hands and knees."

"What did she say?" asked the friend.

The husband replied, "She said, 'Come out from under that bed, you coward!'"

Moo-shoe pork

Another Old Favorite

Sweet & Sour Pork

Everyone's favorite. Use the same recipe for sweet & sour chicken or shrimp by just substituting for the pork. Add sliced red cherries if you want added color.

Ingredients:

- 1 pound boneless pork (I like to use pork loin, but some like pork butt)
- 1 egg, lightly beaten
- 1 teaspoon salt
- ¼ cup cornstarch
- ¼ cup flour
- ¼ cup chicken stock
- 3 cups peanut oil for frying

Sauce:

- 1 tablespoon peanut oil
- 1 teaspoon finely chopped garlic
- 1 large green pepper, seeded and cut into ½ inch squares
- 1 medium carrot scarped and sliced into 2 inch strips ¼ inch wide and ¼ inch thick
- 1 20 0unce can of pineapple chunks
- ½ cup chicken stock
- 4 tablespoon sugar
- 4 tablespoon red wine vinegar
- 1 teaspoon soy sauce
- 1 tablespoon cornstarch dissolved in 2 tablespoon of water

Directions:

Trim any excess fat from the pork and cut the meat into bite-sized pieces.

In a large bowl, mix together the egg, ¼ cup of cornstarch, ¼ cup of flour, ¼ cup chicken stock and salt. Make sure all the ingredients for the sauce are in easy reach.

Preheat the oven to 250° F.

Add the pork to the egg and flour mixture, and stir to ensure all the meat is evenly coated.

In a large wok or deep fryer, heat the 3 cups of peanut oil to 375° F. Individually drop pieces of pork into the heated oil (I do about 8 pieces at a time) until the pork floats to the surface and is a crisp deep golden brown. Be careful not to burn them. Adjust the heat if necessary. When done, remove the pork with a slotted spoon or strainer and place on a wire rack to let drain for a few minutes. Then add the cooked pork to an oven proof baking dish and put in the oven to keep warm. Do the same with the remainder of the pork and add it to the first batch.

Open the can of pineapple, drink the pineapple juice and set the rest aside.

While the pork is in the oven, make the sauce by setting a wok or 10" skillet over high heat for a good 30 seconds until very hot. Add the tablespoon of oil, swirl it around to coat the pan and continue to heat until the oil starts to smoke. Lower the heat to medium high. Add the garlic, then the green pepper and the carrot. Stir-fry for 2 or 3 minutes until the vegetables slightly darken and turn a rich color. Do not let them burn. Combine the chicken stock, vinegar, soy sauce and sugar then add it to the wok and bring to a boil. Continue boiling for about 1 minute or until all the sugar is dissolved. Give the cornstarch/water mixture a quick stir to recombine it and add it to the pan. Cook, stirring constantly, until the sauce becomes thick and clear. Now add the pineapple and the pork and continue to cook until the pineapple is heated through and serve immediately.

Serves 4 as an entrée.

Sweet and Sour Pork

At a traffic court, the judge asked the motorist: Tell me, why did you park your car here?

The man said: "Well, there was a sign that said "fine for parking.

Baked Haddock

My New England roots show with this baked haddock recipe. There is something special about good cold-water fish. If you want, you can also use the stuffing from the Baked Stuffed Shrimp (see recipe) instead of the breadcrumb mixture.

Ingredients

- 1½ lbs haddock
- ¾ cup milk (for soaking the fish in) (optional)
- 6 tablespoons butter
- 2 tablespoons onions, chopped fine
- 1 garlic clove, minced
- ¼ cup dry sherry
- 1 tablespoon dried parsley
- 1 dash paprika
- Salt, to taste
- ½ cup breadcrumbs
- ½ cup crushed butter flavored cracker (such as Ritz or Townhouse)

Directions

Preheat oven to 350°F. Rinse fish and then soak in milk (This will take away any "fishiness"). Melt the butter in a small frying pan. Add the onion and sauté until softened, then add garlic and continue to sauté for another minute.

Remove from heat; add the sherry, parsley, paprika and salt to taste.

Mix the breadcrumbs with crushed cracker crumbs.

Remove the fish from the milk, rinse again, and then place in a baking dish. Pour the crumb mixture over fish, and then pour butter/sherry mixture over the crumbs.

Bake at 350°F for about 25 minutes. If desired, place under broiler on high until golden brown and slightly crispy. (Watch it closely; this does not take long to cook).

What do you call a fish with no eyes? A fsh.

Scallop Crepe Dinner

The same dish can be made with shrimp or a good white fish instead of the scallops.

Ingredients:

- 1½ pounds of sea scallops
- 12 Basic Dinner Crepes (see recipe)
- 2 tablespoons light cream
- Mornay Sauce (see recipe)

Preparations:

Bring 4 cups of water to a boil and add 2 teaspoons of salt. Add the scallops and bring back to a boil. Reduce the heat, cover and let simmer for 2 minutes. Drain the scallops and slice each in half to make ¼ - ½ inch thick medallions.

Prepare the Mornay sauce according to the recipe except use 1½ cups of cream instead of just the 1 cup called for. Stir in the scallops.

Spoon about ¼ of the mixture down the center of a crepe, brown side down and roll up. Place the filled crepe, seam side down, in a baking dish large enough to accommodate all the crepes. Stir 2 teaspoons of crème into the remaining filling and spoon over the crepes. Cover and bake a 375° F for 25 minutes. This is great with asparagus on the side covered with some of the sauce.

Serves 6.

Just spent $300 on a limousine and discovered that the fee doesn't include a driver...

Can't believe I've spent all that money and have nothing to chauffeur it!

Scallop Crepe Dinner with Asparagus

A woman has twins, and gives them up for adoption. One of them goes to a family in Egypt and is named "Amal." The other goes to a family in Spain; they name him "Juan."

Years later, Juan sends a picture of himself to his mom. Upon receiving the picture, she tells her husband that she wishes she also had a picture of Amal.

Her husband responds, "But they are twins if you've seen Juan, you've seen Amal."

Baked Stuffed Shrimp

I think that the stuffing in this recipe is to die for! I have trouble refraining from eating too much before I stuff the shrimp! You can use it as a stuffing for other seafood such as stuffed haddock, cod or Pollack. The recipe calls for 8-15 ct. shrimp, but 5 ct. would be much better. Plan on one, two or three shrimp per person, depending on size.

Ingredients:

- 2 shallots, finely chopped
- 3 cloves garlic, minced
- 3 tablespoons finely chopped fresh parsley leaves
- 3 tablespoons unsalted butter
- ½ pound scallops, chopped
- 1/3 cup chicken broth/stock
- ¼ cup dry white wine or Sherry
- 32 Ritz crackers crushed into coarse crumbs
- 3 tablespoons butter, melted
- 8-12 jumbo shrimp (8/15 ct), about 1 ½ pounds
- 2 tablespoons unsalted butter
- ¼ teaspoon paprika

Directions:

Preheat oven to 375°F. and butter a large baking dish.

For the Stuffing:

In a large heavy skillet cook shallots, garlic, and parsley in unsalted butter over moderate heat, stirring occasionally, for 1 to 2 minutes. Add scallops and wine and cook stirring for about 3 minutes, until the wine reduces by half. Stir in broth and cracker crumbs and cook for 1 minute more making sure there is enough liquid to keep the mixture together, and remove skillet from heat.

Prepared Stuffing

Peel and devein the shrimp, leaving tail intact. Butterfly by cutting along the inside of the curve almost, but not quite, through the shrimp.

Mound about 2 tablespoons of the stuffing onto each shrimp, pressing gently, and put shrimp, stuffed sides up, in baking dish. Melt butter and drizzle over the shrimp. Sprinkle the shrimp with paprika and bake 20 minutes, or until stuffing is golden. Garnish shrimp with parsley and serve with lemon wedges.

Stuffed Shrimp ready to be baked

Baked Stuffed Shrimp, the finished product

Lobster Newberg

This ritzy dish is very expensive in restaurants yet it is so simple to do at home. But the lobster is still expensive.

Ingredients:

- 6 tablespoons butter
- 1 ½ cups light cream
- ½ pound Lobster meat (or more)
- 2 teaspoon lemon juice
- Paprika
- 2 tablespoons flour
- 3 egg yolks, beaten
- 3 tablespoons dry sherry
- ¼ teaspoon salt
- Patty shells or toast cups

Directions:

Melt the butter in skillet. Add in the flour and whisk well to create a roux. Add the cream all at once and cook, stirring constantly, until the sauce thickens and bubbles and all the floury taste is gone. Stir a small amount of the hot mixture into the beaten egg yolks to heat up the eggs so they won't cook when added to the cream. Return that mixture to the hot cream mixture and cook, stirring, constantly, until mixture thickens. Add the lobster and continue cooking until the lobster is heated. Add the sherry, lemon juice, and salt to taste. Sprinkle with paprika. Serve in patty shells or toast cups.

Serves 2.

Lobster Newberg

A group of friars were behind on their belfry payments, so they opened up a small florist shop to raise funds. Since everyone liked to buy flowers from the men of God, a rival florist across town thought the competition was unfair. He asked the good fathers to close down, but they would not.

He went back and begged the friars to close. They ignored him. So, the Rival florist hired Hugh MacTaggart, the roughest and most vicious thug in town to 'persuade' them to close. Hugh beat up the friars and trashed their store, saying he'd be back if they didn't close up shop. Terrified, they did so, thereby proving that "Hugh, and only Hugh can prevent florist friars".

Pan Roasted Swordfish

Swordfish is one of my favorite fish and this dish is really easy to prepare. Try to use fresh swordfish rather than frozen. It's worth the effort.

Ingredients:

- 4 1-inch thick swordfish fillets (about 6 ounces each)
- ¼ cup (1/2 stick) butter at room temperature
- 2 teaspoons chopped fresh parsley
- 1 garlic cloves, minced
- ½ teaspoon lemon peel, or 1 teaspoon of lemon juice.
- ½ teaspoon freshly ground pepper plus extra for sprinkling
- Salt for sprinkling
- ¼ cup white wine
- 1 tablespoon olive oil

Directions:

Preheat the over to 400° F. Meanwhile, in a small bowl, mash together the butter, parsley, garlic, pepper, lemon. Add salt to taste. Set aside.

Heat the oil in a heavy ovenproof skillet over medium high heat until oil is shimmering. Sprinkle both sides of the swordfish with salt and pepper and place the swordfish in the skillet. Let cook until the underside is browned, about 3 minutes. Turn the swordfish over; add the wine to the skillet and transfer to the oven. Roast until cooked through, about 10 minutes. Transfer the swordfish to plates.

Add the seasoned butter mixture to the same hot skillet. Cook over medium high heat, stirring and scraping up the browned bits until melted and bubbling. Do not let it burn.

Pour the butter sauce over the swordfish and serve.

Serves 4.

Pan Roasted Swordfish right from the oven

Pan Roasted Swordfish plated

Swordfish with Rosemary and Wine Sauce

I simply adore swordfish. I usually just broil it with butter and serve with lemon. But, even when you really love something, you can always find some variation that makes it better. So, voilà! Here is a very tasty variation.

Ingredients:

- 4 6-ounce swordfish steaks (each 1 to 1 1/2 inches thick)
- 2 tablespoons olive oil
- 2 ½ teaspoons chopped fresh rosemary
- 6 tablespoons minced shallots
- 6 tablespoons dry white wine (Sauvignon Blanc my favorite)
- 3 tablespoons fresh lemon juice
- ½ cup (1 stick) chilled butter, cut into 8 pieces

Directions:

Prepare barbecue (medium-high heat) or broiler. Brush fish with oil. Sprinkle with 2 teaspoons rosemary. Season with salt and pepper.

Combine shallots, wine and lemon juice in small saucepan. Boil until liquid is reduced to 2 tablespoons, about 5 minutes. Remove from heat. Add remaining rosemary. Add 1 piece of butter; whisk until melted. Place pan over low heat; add remaining butter, 1 piece at a time, whisking until each piece melts before adding the next. Remove from heat. Season with salt and pepper to taste.

Meanwhile, grill/broil the fish until opaque in center, about 3 minutes per side. Plate the swordfish; pour the rosemary-white wine sauce to cover the fish and serve.

Serves 4.

"A balanced diet is one cookie in each hand."

-Barbara Johnson

Shrimp Lo Mein

This Lo Mein also works well with chicken, pork, beef, just vegetables, or almost anything you can think of. This can be a main dish or a side dish for a multi-dish oriental meal. In Chinese restaurants, this is usually treated as a side dish. I do this version is a full meal.

Ingredients:

- 1 cup shrimp stock, chicken stock or vegetable broth
- ½ cup low sodium soy sauce
- 3 tablespoons cornstarch
- 1 tablespoon oyster sauce
- ½ teaspoon ground ginger
- 8 ounces of lo mein noodles or wide fettuccine
- 1 tablespoon sesame oil
- 2 tablespoons peanut oil
- 1 ½ pounds medium shrimp, shelled and deveined
- 4 scallions, cut into 1 inch pieces
- 3 cloves garlic, minced
- 8 ounces snap (snow) peas
- 1 large sweet red pepper, cut into 1 inch pieces or strips
- 1 ½ cups fresh bean sprouts

Directions:

In small bowl, whisk together the stock, soy sauce, cornstarch, oyster sauce and ginger and set aside.

Cook fettuccine according to instructions until al dente; drain and toss with the sesame oil making sure all the noodles are covered with the sesame oil. Set aside.

Heat wok over high heat. Add 1 tablespoon of peanut oil and heat until it just starts to smoke. Add shrimp and stir-fry until pink, about 2 to 3 minutes, then remove with slotted spoon and set aside.

Reduce heat to medium; add remaining oil to the wok. Add the scallions, garlic, snap peas and peppers; stir-fry about 3 minutes. Add stock/soy mixture and stir-fry until the sauce starts to thicken and then cook for 30 seconds longer.

Add in sprouts and mix; then fettuccine and mix, and then the shrimp. Mix thoroughly to coat and heat thoroughly, about 1 minute. Serve immediately.

Serves 6 as a main course and 12 as a side dish.

Shrimp Lo Mein
(also on back cover)

I once heard a joke about amnesia, but I forgot how it goes.

Garlic Butter Salmon

This Garlic Butter Salmon is an ultra-easy and flavorful dinner.
It's ready in less than 30 minutes; serve with salads and roasted veggies.

Ingredients:

- 1 1/4 pound salmon
- 2 tablespoons lemon juice
- 2 cloves garlic, minced
- 3 tablespoons melted butter
- 1/2 teaspoon salt
- 1/4 teaspoon black pepper
- 1/4 teaspoon oregano
- 1/4 crushed red pepper
- 1 tablespoon chopped parsley — for garnishing

Directions:

Preheat oven to 375 degrees.

Line a baking sheet with foil. The piece of foil should be big enough to fold over and completely cover and seal the fish.

In a small bowl, add lemon juice, garlic, and melted butter. Whisk everything together.

Place the salmon on the prepared baking sheet. Pour the butter mixture over the salmon. Season with salt, pepper, oregano, and red pepper flakes.

Fold the sides of the foil over the salmon. Make sure it is well sealed so the sauce does not leak.

Place into oven and bake until cooked for about 12-16 minutes.

Open the foil and **broil** the fish for 2-3 minutes. Be careful not to burn the fish!

Remove from the oven and plate the fish. Using a spoon, pour some of the butter sauce left in the foil onto the salmon before serving.

Garnish with parsley and serve.

Garlic Butter Salmon after baking, before broiling

A cantor, the man who sings the prayers at a synagogue, brags before his congregation in a booming, bellowing voice: "Two years ago I insured my voice with Lloyds of London for $750,000."

There is a hushed and awed silence in the crowded room.

Suddenly, from the back of the room, the quiet, nasal voice of an elderly woman is heard, "So what did you do with the money?"

Honey Stir Fried Shrimp

If you still happen to have shrimp left over from the big block you bought to save money …

Ingredients:

- 1 to 1½ pounds shrimp (16-24 count), peeled and deveined
- 1 tablespoon peanut or vegetable oil
- 4 cloves garlic, minced
- 2 teaspoons fresh gingerroot, grated or minced
- 1 sweet red pepper, seeded and diced
- 1 cup fresh snow peas
- 3 green onions, chopped
- Cooked rice or noodles

Sauce:

- ½ cup honey
- 1/3 cup soy sauce
- 1½ tablespoons cider vinegar
- 1 tablespoon cornstarch
- 1 tablespoon orange zest

Directions:

Make the sauce by combining all the sauce ingredients in a bowl. Mix until smooth. Set aside.

Heat the oil in wok or large fry pan over medium-high heat. Add the garlic and ginger and sauté for 1 minute. Add the diced pepper and snow peas and stir-fry for 1 minute or until tender-crisp.

Add the shrimp; stir-fry just until shrimp turns pink (about 1 minute).

Add the sauce. Cook, stirring constantly, until the mixture comes to a boil and thickens. Stir in the green onions.

Serve over cooked rice or noodles.

A hangover is the wrath of grapes.

Shrimp Scampi with Saghetti

This is yet another shrimp recipe. Shrimp Scampi is one of the easiest and most popular recipes anywhere.

Ingredients:

- 1½ pounds large shrimp, about 20, shelled and deveined (16 to 24 ct works best)
- 1 pound thin spaghetti, linguini, or whatever type desired
- 4 tablespoons butter
- 4 tablespoons extra virgin olive oil
- 5 garlic cloves, minced
- 1 large shallot, finely diced
- a pinch of red pepper flakes (optional)
- ½ cup of a good dry white wine
- 2 tablespoons lemon juice, fresh if possible
- ¼ cup of finely chopped fresh parsley
- Kosher salt and ground black pepper

Directions:

For the pasta, on the stove bring a large pot of water to a boil. When it comes to a boil add 2 tablespoons of salt and the pasta. Stir to make sure the pasta separates. Cook until al dente, about 6 to 8 minutes and then drain.

While the pasta is cooking, in a large skillet melt 2 tablespoons of butter and 2 tablespoons of olive oil over medium high heat. Sauté the shallots, garlic and pepper flakes about 3 to 4 minutes until the shallots become translucent. Season the shrimp with salt and pepper and add them to the skillet and cook until they turn pink turning the shrimp once, about 2 to 3 minutes. Remove the shrimp to a plate to keep warm. Add the wine and lemon juice to the skillet and bring to a boil. Add the remaining 2 tablespoons of butter and 2 tablespoons of oil. When the butter has melted, return the shrimp to the skillet along with the parsley and cooked spaghetti. Mix well and season with salt and pepper to taste. You may drizzle more olive oil over each dish and serve immediately.

Serves 4 to 6.

Shrimp Scampi with Spaghetti

*A lady went into a grocery store and asked for 50 gallons of milk. The clerk, amazed,
asked her what she was going to do with that much milk.
I have a skin problem and the doctor prescribed a milk bath.
The clerk asked, "Pasteurized?"
She replied, "No, just up to my chin."*

Shrimp and Squid Stuffed Squid

Squid isn't very flavorful on its own. So, stuff it with flavor and cook it in tomato gravy to excite your taste buds.

Ingredients:

- 1 tablespoon olive oil
- ¼ cup finely chopped onion
- ½ teaspoon Kosher salt
- 2 cloves garlic, finely minced
- 8 to 10 whole squid, tubes about 5 or 6 inches in length
- 3 ounces raw shrimp, shelled and de-veined
- ¼ cup breadcrumbs
- 2 tablespoons finely chopped tomato
- 2 teaspoons lemon zest
- 2 teaspoons finely chopped fresh ginger
- 1 teaspoon fresh parsley leaves, chopped
- ¼ teaspoon freshly ground black pepper
- 2 cups prepared tomato gravy (see recipe)

Directions:

Preheat an oven to 375° F.

Heat the olive oil in a medium sauté pan over medium heat until shimmering. Add the onions and salt and sauté until the onions turn translucent, about 1 to 2 minutes. Do not brown. Add the garlic and continue to cook for another minute. Transfer the mixture to a medium mixing bowl and set aside to cool.

Clean the squid thoroughly and remove the heads from the tentacles and discard the heads. Better yet, buy them already cleaned and separated. If possible, turn the tubes inside out (since the outside skin tends to curl outward, it'll hold the stuffing better inside out), put into a bowl and set in the refrigerator until ready to use.

Place the tentacles and the shrimp into the bowl of a food processor and pulse 6 to 8 times or until there are no large pieces visible. <u>Do not process until smooth.</u> Transfer to the mixing bowl along with the onions and garlic. Add the breadcrumbs, tomato, lemon zest, ginger, parsley and pepper. Stir to combine well.

Place the mixture into a pastry bag with a tip just small enough to fit into the end of the tubes, or you may use a resealable freezer bag and snip 1 corner and put a pastry tip through the hole. Pipe the stuffing into the tubes, dividing the mixture evenly between them. <u>Do not over-stuff.</u> Overstuffing will cause the tubes to split as the stuffing expands during cooking.

Place the tubes into an 8 by 11-inch glass baking dish or oven-tempered pan and cover with the tomato gravy. Cover tightly with aluminum foil and bake for 30 minutes

Serve on you favorite pasta.

Stuffed Squid in the Pan

Stuffed Squid with Angel Hair Pasta

Scallops Provencal

This is another old favorite. Simple to make, and always elegant.

Ingredients:

- 1 pound large fresh sea scallops*
- Kosher salt and freshly ground black pepper
- All-purpose flour, for dredging
- 4 tablespoons (½ stick) unsalted butter, divided
- ½ cup chopped shallots (2 large)
- 1 garlic clove, minced
- ¼ cup chopped fresh flat-leaf parsley leaves
- 1/3 cup dry white wine
- 1 lemon, cut in half

* Do not necessarily buy the scallops by weight since they have a large water content. Buy them by size figuring many you will need per serving.

Directions:

Cut off the small muscle on each scallop if present.

If too large, cut each of the scallops in half horizontally. Sprinkle with salt and pepper, toss with flour, and shake off the excess.

In a very large sauté pan, heat 2 tablespoons of the butter over high heat until sizzling and add the scallops in a single layer not too close together. Lower the heat to medium and allow the scallops to brown lightly on 1 side <u>without moving them</u>, then turn and brown lightly on the other side. This should take 3 to 4 minutes, total. Melt the rest of the butter in the pan with the scallops. Add the shallots, garlic, and parsley and sauté for 2 more minutes, tossing the seasonings with the scallops. Add the wine, cook for 1 minute, and taste for seasoning. Serve hot with a squeeze of lemon juice.

Scallops Provencal

Back in the 1800's the Tates Watch Company of Massachusetts wanted to produce other products and, since they already made the cases for pocket watches, decided to market compasses for the pioneers traveling west. It turned out that although their watches were of finest quality, their compasses were so bad that people often ended up in Canada or Mexico rather than California. This, of course, is the origin of the expression; "He who has a Tates is lost!"

Shrimp with Snow Peas and Water Chestnuts

Here is a different Oriental meal, not one that you would often think of, but, try it, you'll like it!

Ingredients:

- 1 pound shrimp, peeled and deveined (large shrimp should be sliced lengthwise)
- Pinch of salt
- 2 tablespoons dry sherry
- 1 tablespoon Peanut Oil, for stir-frying
- 1 tablespoon minced fresh ginger
- ½ pound snow peas, stems and strings removed
- ½ cup sliced water chestnuts
- 1 tablespoon soy sauce
- ½ teaspoon cornstarch, dissolved in ¼ cup water or stock

Directions:

Place the shrimp in a large bowl and sprinkle with salt. Add the sherry and marinate for 20 minutes to several hours.

Drain the shrimp and reserve marinade. Heat the wok over high heat; add the oil. Add the ginger and stir-fry until fragrant. Add the shrimp and stir-fry until shrimp are pink on all sides (2 to 4 minutes, depending on size).

Add the snow peas and water chestnuts and stir-fry until just heated through. Add the reserved marinade, soy sauce, and cornstarch mixture. Bring to a boil and cook until sauce thickens. Serve immediately with rice.

Yield: Serves 2 to 4 as main course or 4 to 6 with other dishes.

She was only a whiskey maker, but he loved her still.

Mom's Seafood Casserole

Many years ago, my mother made this totally awesome seafood casserole, but unfortunately, she never wrote down the recipe. Over the years I have tried to duplicate it, but with little success. This is as close as I've come so far. I'm still lookin' ma!

Ingredients:

- 2 cups cooked rice
- 8 tablespoons (1 stick) butter
- ½ cup. Flour (8 tablespoons)
- 2 cups. Milk
- ½ teaspoon tarragon, crushed
- ¼ cup dry Sherry
- ¾ lbs. fresh shrimp, peeled and deveined (31/35 count are a good size)
- ¾ lbs. fresh sea scallops
- ¾ lbs. fresh lobster meat (about 1 ¼ pound live lobster)
- ½ cup Parmesan cheese
- 1 ½ cups Mozzarella cheese

Directions:

Cook the rice. In a medium saucepan, bring 2 cups of water to a boil. Add the rice and mix well. Cover the pan and lower the heat the lowest simmer temperature. Cook covered for 20 minutes. Remove lid and stir to make sure the rice is done. Cover and set aside to cool.

If you have a live lobster, cook it in boiling water and when cool, extract all the meat, slice into good-sized chunks and place in a bowl. Slice the scallops into ¼ inch medallions and place in separate bowl. Place the shrimp in a third bowl. You now have 3 bowls of seafood. Set them all aside.

Preheat oven to 350° F.

Make white sauce:

Make a roux by melting the butter in a large saucepan or Dutch oven, large enough to hold all the ingredients, over low heat. After melted, add the flour and cook for about 3 minutes stirring continuously until blended and the mixture gets a nutty aroma. Slowly add in milk and stir until sauce is smooth and thickened, stirring constantly. (Add more milk or flour to adjust thickness.) Add the tarragon and stir until blended in, then add the Sherry and blend again until smooth. The sauce should be fairly thick.

Final Steps:

Mix together white sauce and rice. Stir in desired seafood, one bowl at a time, and cheeses, saving some cheese for topping. Place all in greased baking dish(es) (Pam spray may be used). Some of the seafood casserole can be frozen for another time. Bake in oven for 30 minutes or until bubbly and cheese starts to brown.

Mom's Seafood Casserole

"The most remarkable thing about my mother is that for 30 years she served the family nothing but leftovers. The original meal has never been found." – Calvin Trillin

Stir-Fried Shrimp In Lobster Sauce

Don't be confused. There is no lobster in lobster sauce. The name comes from the sauce that is used to prepare Lobster Cantonese. But it is so good! The sauce recipe is also separate in the Sauce section.

Ingredients:

- 1 pound medium shrimp, shelled and deveined
- 5 tablespoons peanut oil
- 6 ounces of fresh shitake mushrooms, sliced
- 4 ounces fresh snow peas
- 4 ounces lean ground pork
- 1 tablespoon sherry
- 2 teaspoons Chinese black bean sauce
- 1 teaspoon finely chopped garlic
- 1 tablespoon low-sodium soy sauce
- 1 teaspoon salt
- ¼ teaspoon sugar
- A touch fresh ground pepper
- 1 whole scallion, both white and green parts, finely chopped
- 1 cup chicken stock
- 2 tablespoons cornstarch mixed in 3 tablespoons chicken stock or water

Directions:

Set a large wok or skillet over high heat for about 30 seconds. Add 2 tablespoon of oil and swirl around pan to coat. When the oil starts to smoke, lower the heat to medium high. Add the shrimp and stir-fry until the shrimp turn pink. Add the sherry and mix well then remove the shrimp to a plate or bowl.

Add 1 tablespoon of oil to the pan. When the oil starts to smoke, add the snow peas and stir-fry until they turn a bright green, about 1 minute. Remove and place with the shrimp. Now stir-fry the mushrooms for 1 minute. Remove and add to the shrimp and snow peas.

Add the last 2 tablespoons of oil to the pan and heat as previous. Add the black bean sauce and garlic and stir-fry for a few seconds to heat thoroughly being careful not to burn the garlic. Add the ground pork and stir-fry until the pork is no longer pink. Add the soy sauce, salt, pepper, sugar, scallions, the reserved shrimp, snow peas and mushrooms and stir to mix. Add the chicken stock, cover and bring to a boil. Stir the cornstarch mixture to recombine and add it to the pan. Stir constantly until the sauce thickens. Serve at once plain or on a bed of rice Serves 4.

Spaghetti with White Clam Sauce

My grandmother, the one on the Italian side of the family, used to make this for me all the time when we would come for a visit. I still love in now just as much as then.

Ingredients:

- 1 pound of spaghetti or linguini
- ¼ cup extra-virgin olive oil
- 4 cloves of garlic, crushed
- ½ cup dry white wine
- 2 cans of chopped clams with juice
- ¼ cup of fresh chopped parsley
- 1 teaspoon of red pepper flakes (or to taste)
- Grated parmesan cheese
- Salt and pepper to taste

Directions:

Cook the pasta according to the box directions.

While the pasta is cooking, put the oil, garlic, and red pepper in a large skillet set on medium low heat. Do not brown the garlic.

Add the wine and clam juice and bring to a boil for about 5 minutes until the liquid starts to reduce.

Turn off the heat, add the clams and mix while still on the burner. Let the sauce sit while the pasta cooks.

Drain the pasta when it is done, add it to the sauce and add the parsley. Mix well and let sit for 5 minutes.

Sprinkle each serving with parmesan cheese.

Spaghetti with White Clam Sauce

"My wife and I were happy for twenty years. Then we met."

-Rodney Dangerfield

Teriyaki Tuna Steak

Quick and simple. Fresh tuna is nothing like what you get in a sandwich from a can.

Ingredients:

- 1 pound fresh tuna steak, like yellow fin

Teriyaki Marinade:

- ¼ cup dark soy sauce
- ¼ cup Mirin (sweetened sake)
- 1 tablespoon sugar

Directions:

Add all the ingredients for the marinade into a bowl and stir until all the sugar has been dissolved into the liquid. Place the tuna (you may cut the tuna into two equally sized pieces if desired) in a 1 quart sized zip lock plastic zip-lock freezer bag. Pour in the marinade and seal the bag. Put the bag in the refrigerator and let marinade for from 30 minutes to an hour, turning the bag once or twice to insure equal coating.

Heat the barbeque grill on high for at least 15 minutes to allow the grate to get very hot. Place the tuna on the grill and coot for 2 to 3 minutes per side, depending on the thickness of the tuna. The tuna should be dark with nice grill marks on the outside and have a raw center. Once placed on the grill, do not move the tuna or you will not get the nice grill marks. If you want the tuna cooked more, lower the heat to medium high when cooking and cook for a minute longer per side. This can also be oven broiled if you wish.

Serves 2.

Teriyaki Tuna Steak with Stir-Fried Snow Peas and Mushrooms (see recipe)

One night at the dinner table, the wife commented, "When we were first married, you took the small piece of steak and gave me the larger. Now you take the large one and leave me the smaller. You don't love me any more?"

"Nonsense, darling," replied the husband, "you just cook better now."

Toasted Spaghetti with Shrimp

Toasted spaghetti is always a novelty. Use it in a variety of other recipes, but try this one first.

Ingredients:

- 3 tablespoons extra-virgin olive oil
- ¾ pound spaghetti broken in half
- 2 to 3 cloves of garlic, minced (to taste)
- A pinch of crushed red pepper (to taste)
- 1 ½ cups water
- 20 ounces bottled clam broth
- 15-24 large shrimp (I like 16/24 count), peeled and deveined
- ¼ cup minced fresh parsley

Directions:

In a deep skillet, heat the oil until shimmering. Add the spaghetti and cook over moderate heat, moving the spaghetti constantly, until golden, about 3 minutes. Add the garlic and a pinch of red pepper, to taste, and cook until fragrant, about 1 minute. Add the clam broth and the water and bring to a boil. Cover and cook over moderate heat until almost al dente, about 8 minutes. Be very careful not to let the spaghetti burn on the bottom of the pan.

This recipe can be modified to use clams. Use 3-dozen littleneck clams instead of the shrimp. Place the cleaned clams in the pasta a few minutes earlier than for the shrimp and cook until all the clams open. Also reduce the amount of water to just 1 cup.

Toasting the Spaghetti

Nestle the shrimp into the pasta, cover and cook until the pasta is al dente, about 5 minutes. If the pasta is too dry, add a few tablespoons of water. Stir in the parsley and serve. Serves 4.

Toasted Spaghetti and Shrimp

*One day, a man from the Czech Republic came to visit his friend in New York.
When asked what he wanted to see, the visitor replied, "I would like to see one of the zoos in America."*

To his delight, the New Yorker took him to the Bronx Zoo. They were touring the zoo, and standing in front of the gorilla cage, when one of the gorillas busted out of the cage and swallowed the Czech whole.

Shocked, his friend from New York quickly called over the zookeeper. He quickly explained the situation and the zookeeper immediately took steps to save the man's friend. The zookeeper got an axe and asked the man, "OK, which gorilla did it? Was it the male or the female?" The New Yorker pointed out the female as the culprit. Quickly, the zookeeper split the female gorilla open and found nothing of the Czech.

He looked at the man from New York, who shrugged and said, "Guess the Czech is in the male."

Shrimp Stuffed Potatoes

This is a truly wonderful dish. Use a full potato for a main dish
or use half a potato as a side. The recipe calls for 6 potatoes, but reduce all the ingredients
proportionally depending on how many people you intend to serve.

Ingredients:

- 6 large Idaho potatoes
- Vegetable oil or butter, for coating potatoes
- 8 tablespoons butter
- 2 cups grated cheddar cheese, plus more for sprinkling
- 2 cups grated Monterey Jack
- 2 cups sour cream
- Salt and pepper to taste
- 1 pound shrimp, peeled and sauteed
- Paprika

Directions:

Preheat oven to 350 degrees.

Wash the potatoes; dry them, and gently pricking them several times with a fork on the sides. Coat each potato with vegetable oil or butter, place on foil covered pan or cookie sheet, and bake for approximately 1 hour.

Place the butter in a large bowl. Remove the potatoes from the oven and carefully slice each potato in half length-wise. Gently scoop out the potato from each half and place in the bowl leaving the potato shells intact.

Using a mixer on high, mix the potatoes, butter, sour cream, salt, and pepper until smooth. Fold in the shrimp and both cheeses into the mixture. Gently stuff the mixture back into the potato shells, making sure not to break the shells. Pile the mixture as high as you can on top of the potato shells. There will probably be extra filling left which can be refrigerated and used in some ingenious creation later or just bake in a small bowl.

Sprinkle each potato with cheese and paprika for color. Bake in the oven for approximately 20 to 30 minutes until browned on top.

Serve while still hot.

Shrimp Stuffed Potatoes

A young missionary on his first term in Africa is out away from camp having devotions in a quiet clearing, as was his custom. This one particular day, while reading his Bible, a lion comes and lies down right beside him, so close that the hot warm smell of his breath is wafting over him. He is, as you would suppose, exceedingly uneasy. He closes his eyes, praying ... but when he opens them, he sees another lion approach from the brush, which proceeds to lie down on the other side of him.

Convinced as he is that this is a test of his faith, he determines to return to his Bible reading. As soon as he does so, the two lions pounce upon him and devour him.

Moral of the story: Don't read between the lions.

Eggplant Parmesan

This is probably the most popular main dish I am asked to make.

Ingredients:

- 2 medium sized eggplant
- My Spaghetti Gravy (see recipe)
- 8 or more ounces Mozzarella cheese, fresh Mozzarella is the best
- Grated Parmesan cheese
- 2 cups Italian bread crumbs
- 4 eggs, beaten
- 1 ½ cups flour
- Olive oil for frying
- Salt and pepper to taste

Directions:

Cut off the ends and discard of the eggplant and discard. With a peeler, peel off all the skin (this is optional, some people like the skin on). Slice the eggplant lengthwise about ¼ inch thick (you decide since there will be some shrinkage when cooked).

Eggplant sliced

Place the flour and breadcrumbs in two separate deep dishes. Place the eggs in a 3rd deep dish or wide bowl. In turn, take each cutlet and dredge it in the flour making sure that the entire cutlet is covered. Shake off the excess. Next, dredge the cutlet in the eggs and let the excess drip off back into the bowl. Place the eggplant in the bowl with the breadcrumbs, making sure to cover every part of the cutlet. Shake off excess and place the breaded eggplant on a clean plate. Repeat for 2 or 3 pieces at a time.

Pour enough olive oil into a large skillet to about ¼ inch and heat over med heat. When the oil is very hot, place as many breaded eggplant pieces as can fit in the skillet leaving about ½ inch between each. Cook over moderate heat until the bottoms of the are a deep golden brown. Turn over the cutlets and cook the other side. While this batch is cooking, bread the next several eggplant pieces. When the current batch is done, place cooked eggplant on a brown paper bag, or the like, to drain.

Eggplant Frying

In a deep pie plate, Corning Ware casserole or similar, place a thin layer of "sauce" followed by a layer of eggplant, another thin layer of sauce, a layer of mozzarella cheese, either sliced or grated, followed by another thin layer of sauce and repeat to the depth desired.

Bake at 350 degrees, uncovered, for 30 minutes or until you see the sauce bubbling, but don't let the top burn.

You can make this recipe ahead of time for future use. Before baking, tightly cover the cooking dish with foil and freeze. You can keep it frozen for weeks before you use it. Just let it defrost before you bake it.

Plated Eggplant Serving

Which is heavier: a litre of water or a litre of butane?

The water.

No matter how much you have, butane will always be a lighter fluid.

Basic Dinner Crepes

Crepes are fun. They are very impressive and you can put almost anything in them to impress guests. Here are just the basics for dinner crepes. Dessert crepes are a bit different and covered in the dessert section.

Basic Crepe Recipe
Ingredients:

- 1 cup flour
- 1½ cups milk
- 2 eggs
- 1 tablespoon vegetable oil
- ¼ teaspoon sugar

Directions:

To make the batter, simply combine all the ingredients in a bowl and mix until there is a smooth fairly thin batter.

There are several ways to cook a crepe. The easiest is to use an electric crepe maker. Just follow the directions that come with the maker.

If you do not have an electric crepe maker, then you can use a 10 inch skillet with a non-stick surface. Heat the skillet over medium heat. To test when the pan is hot enough, sprinkle a few drops of water on the surface. If the water sizzles and bounces, then the pan is ready.

Remove the pan from the heat and holding it with one hand, pour 2 tablespoons of the batter into the pan. Quickly start rotating the pan so that the batter coats the bottom in a thin even layer. Return the skillet to the heat and cook for 45 to 60 seconds.

When the crepe is lightly browned on the bottom, invert the pan and let the crepe drop onto a paper towel. You may need a small spatula to get the crepe started off the pan. Let each crepe cool.

Note that you do not have to cook the crepes on both sides. Just put the filling desired on the un-browned side and roll the crepe as desired, exposing the browned side.

Stack cooled crepes between two layers of waxed paper. Use right away or freeze for up to several weeks before using.

Grilled Lamb Steaks

I like to use lamb steaks cut from the leg. Go to the grocery or butcher and pick out a nice leg of lamb. Have the butcher cut it into ½ - ¾ inch thick steaks (they should do it for no charge). You may broil the lamb in the oven instead of grilling, but grilling is far better.

Ingredients:

- 4 good sized lamb steaks
- 1 tablespoon rosemary
- 1 teaspoon thyme
- 2 cloves garlic, minced
- ½ teaspoon kosher salt
- ¼ teaspoon fresh ground pepper
- ½ cup olive oil

Directions:

Place all the ingredients, except the lamb, into a small food processor and pulse blend unto all the ingredients are well blended. Pour mixture into a large one-gallon plastic zip lock bag. Drop in the lamb, seal the bag, taking out as much air as possible, and move the contents around to coat all the steaks. Place in refrigerator for 4 to 12 hours, turning the bag several times.

Remove the steaks from the refrigerator and allow to come to room temperature, about 30 minutes.

Heat grill to high so that the grill is very hot. Sear the steaks for about 3 minutes per side, or until whatever doneness is desired. Let rest for 2-3 minutes before serving. This is great served with the Peppers and Mushroom side dish (see recipe). Serves 4.

Where did Noah keep the bees? In the ark hives.

SIDES

Noodles Romanoff with Flat-Iron Steak

Stir-Fried Snow Peas and Mushrooms

Ingredients:

- 1 pound fresh snow peas
- 6 to 8 mushrooms, about 1½ to 2 inches in diameter
- ½ cup of sliced Water Chestnuts
- 1½ teaspoons salt
- ½ teaspoon sugar
- 2 tablespoons water
- 2 tablespoons peanut oil, or flavorless vegetable oil

Directions:

Slice the mushrooms into ¼ inch slices, place in a bowl and set aside.

Snap or cut off the tips of the snow peas and remove the strings from the pods.

Set a 10 to 12-inch wok or skillet over high heat for about 30 seconds; pour in the oil and swirl around the pan to coat for another 30 seconds. Turn the heat down to moderate if the oil begins to smoke. Put in the mushrooms and water chestnuts and stir-fry for about 2 minutes. Add the snow peas, salt and sugar and then 2 tablespoons of water. Cook over high heat for another 2 minutes or until the water has evaporated. Transfer the contents to a heated platter and serve at once.

"Doc, I can't stop singing 'The Green, Green Grass of Home.'"

"That sounds like Tom Jones Syndrome."

"Is it common?"

"It's Not Unusual."

Sautéed Mushrooms

This is my favorite steak topping, although I do like them as just a side to almost anything.

Ingredients:

- 8 to 10 ounces button mushrooms
- 2 tablespoons extra virgin olive oil
- 2 tablespoons butter
- 2 cloves garlic, minced
- ¼ cup pale dry sherry
- ½ teaspoon black pepper
- ½ teaspoon salt

Directions:

Clean and slice the mushrooms as desired.

In a large skillet, heat the butter and the olive oil under medium high heat until the oil is shimmering. Sauté the garlic until fragrant. Add the mushrooms and sprinkle with the salt. Stir-fry them until they just start to sweat. Add the sherry and continue to sauté until the sherry is reduced by half. Taste a mushroom and adjust the seasoning as desired. Remove from the heat when the mushrooms are cooked but still firm. Serve on meat or as a side.

I like my mushrooms in a lot of olive oil, so add more during the cooking phase as desired.

Sautéed Mushrooms smothering a nice thick sirloin

Sherlock Holmes turned to Dr Watson and announced: "The murderer lives in the house with the yellow door."

Good grief, Holmes," said Watson. "How on earth did you deduce that?"

"It's a lemon entry, my dear Watson."

5 Spice Steak Fried Rice

Ingredients:

- 2 cups cooked rice
- 1 pound steak, rib eye or sirloin, but any good steak will do
- 4 tablespoon soy sauce
- 2 tablespoon Sherry or Rice Wine
- 2 shallots
- 2 celery stalks
- 4 large cloves of garlic, minced
- 2 tablespoon Oyster Sauce
- 2 teaspoon 5-Spice Powder
- 1 tablespoon Sesame Oil
- ½ teaspoon Cayenne pepper
- ½ teaspoon salt
- Peanut oil to stir fry

Directions:

Trim the fat off the steak and cut thinly into bite sized pieces about 1inch by ½ inch. Place the meat in a bowl. Add 2 tablespoon of soy sauce and the Sherry or wine and mix to coat all the meat. Set aside for about 30 minutes mixing occasionally.

Cut up the shallots and the celery into small pieces, place in a bowl and set aside.

Heat a large wok with 1 tablespoon of peanut oil until it just starts to smoke. Add ¼ of the garlic and stir-fry for just about 10-15 seconds. Be careful not to burn it. Give the steak another quick mix then add ½ the meat to the wok and stir fry until just done. Remove the cooked meat to a bowl. If you are using a steak with a high fat content, there may be a lot of liquid in the bottom of the wok. Try not to transfer any of that with the steak and pour it off after the steak has been removed. Add another tablespoon of oil to the wok and repeat the process with more garlic and the rest of the meat. When done, give the wok a quick wipe with paper towels.

Heat the wok again to high with another tablespoon of peanut oil. Add the celery and shallots and stir-fry for about 30 seconds. Add the remaining garlic and stir-fry for another 30 seconds. Now add back the meat and any accumulated juices, the oyster sauce, 5-Spice powder, Cayenne, sesame oil, salt and remaining soy sauce. Mix well. Now add the rice and continue to mix until all the rice is coated with the sauce. Serve hot. Remainder can be refrigerated and used as leftovers for another day.

Meatballs

This is another recipe you just love to get your hands into. You can use these meatballs as a side with pasta or with a little Provolone cheese in a hoagie for a sandwich. There, you have two recipes on the same page! Some people like to use beef, pork and veal, but I find that all chuck has better flavor.

Ingredients:

- 1 pound ground chuck (or, if you insist, equal amounts of veal, beef and pork)
- 3 eggs
- 1 cup Italian bread crumbs
- ½ cup Pecorino Romano cheese, grated
- 2 garlic cloves, minced
- 1 medium onion finely diced
- ¼ cup fresh parsley, chopped
- 1 teaspoon salt
- 1 teaspoon pepper
- My Spaghetti Gravy (see recipe)

Directions:

Preheat oven to 350° F. Place all the ingredients in a large bowl. Then blend together using both hands (latex gloves optional) until all the ingredients are well mixed together and uniform, usually for about 5 minutes.

Take enough of the mixture to make a single meatball that is 1 ½ to 2 inches in diameter and form a ball in your hands. Do not make the meatballs too small or too large. You can use an ice cream scoop or meatball scoop so that they are all of uniform size. With both hands, roll it into a firm, tight ball. Place the finished meatball on a lightly greased baking sheet or wire rack.

After all the meatballs are rolled, place in the oven and cook for 20 to 25 minutes.

When done, place all the meatballs in a large pot of freshly made tomato gravy and simmer for about 1 hour. This allows the tomato gravy to infuse in the meatballs and also the meatballs to flavor the gravy. Serve immediately or put in the refrigerator to reheat as needed.

Meatballs ready for cooking

As an alternative to baking, and my preferred method, place the uncooked meatballs directly into a large pot of just made hot spaghetti gravy (see recipe in sauces section). Make sure they are all submerged in the gravy and simmer covered, under low heat, for 2 to 3 hours and let stand until cool. Refrigerate overnight. Reheat for use. I personally prefer this method because it enhances the sauce with the wonderful meatball flavor even more than the above recipe.

A gorilla walks into a bar and, to the amazement of the bartender, orders a martini.

When the bartender gives the gorilla the martini, he is further surprised to see that the ape is holding a $20 bill.

The bartender takes the $20 bill, then he decides to see just how smart the gorilla is, so he hands the gorilla $1 change.

The gorilla quietly sips the martini until the bartender breaks the silence.

"We don't get too many apes in here," he says.

The gorilla replies, "At $19 a drink, I'm not surprised."

Pork Fried Rice

Most fried rice dishes use the same basic ingredients. Try variations with beef, chicken, shrimp or just veggies.

Ingredients:

- 2 eggs
- ¼ teaspoon salt
- 1/8 teaspoon black pepper, or to taste
- 5 tablespoons peanut oil for frying, or as needed
- 1 medium onion or two large shallots, chopped or diced
- 1 cup roast pork loin or boneless chops, diced
- 4 cups cold cooked rice
- 2 tablespoons dark soy sauce
- 8 to 12 ounces of fresh bean sprouts (optional)

Directions:

Marinade the pork in your favorite oriental marinade and then roast the pork. Try to keep the meat as moist as possible. Discard the marinade and dice the pork and set aside. Alternately, dice the uncooked pork and stir-fry in the wok with your favorite marinade or sauce.

Lightly beat the eggs. Stir in small amount of salt and pepper.

Heat a wok on medium-high to high heat. Add 1 tablespoon of oil. When oil is hot, pour half the egg mixture and cook over medium heat, swish it around in the wok to make it thin, turning over once. Place the eggs on at plate and when cooled cut into thin strips and pieces, and save for later. Cook the other half the same way.

Turn the heat back to medium-high and add 2 tablespoons oil. When the oil is hot, add the onion. Stir-fry briefly, and then add the pork. Stir-fry until the pork and onion are well cooked. Add the optional bean sprouts and stir-fry for one minute. Remove from the wok.

Add 2 tablespoons oil, turn the heat down to medium, and stir-fry the rice. Separate the individual grains as best you can while stirring. Stir in the dark soy sauce. Add the other ingredients and mix well until the soy covers everything and all is well heated. Season with salt and pepper to taste. Serve while hot. Can be refrigerated for days.

"I like rice. Rice is great if you're hungry for 2000 of something."
– Mitch Hedberg

Sausage Stuffing

I like sausage stuffing at Thanksgiving. I like sausage stuffing with chicken. I like sausage stuffing in turkey sandwiches. I love sausage stuffing.

Ingredients:

- 1 Package of Pepperidge Farm Herb Stuffing (or similar) or 2 loaves Italian bread (2 pounds), crusts removed and bread cut into 3/4-inch cubes (20 cups)
- ¼ cup extra-virgin olive oil
- 1½ pounds sweet Italian sausage, casings removed
- 2 large onions, chopped (fine to medium chop)
- 1 large celery rib, finely diced
- 3 large garlic cloves, very finely chopped
- ¼ cup finely chopped sage leaves
- 4 tablespoons unsalted butter
- 3 cups turkey/chicken stock or low-sodium chicken broth
- Salt and freshly ground pepper

Directions:

If using the cut bread, preheat the oven to 375° F. Spread the bread cubes in a large roasting pan and toast for 15 minutes, stirring occasionally, until dry and lightly browned.

In a large, deep skillet, heat the oil. Add the sausage and cook over moderately high heat, breaking up the meat, until browned and no trace of pink remains. Add the chopped onion, celery and garlic and cook until softened, about 6 minutes. Stir in the sage and butter. Scrape the mixture into a large bowl. Add the bread cubes or stuffing mix and toss. Stir in 2 cups of the stock and season with salt and pepper. Add more stock if the stuffing is too dry, being careful not to make it too moist.

After stuffing the turkey, put the remaining stuffing in a baking dish and drizzle with 1 cup of the stock. Bake for 30 minutes at 375° F, until the stuffing is heated through and crisp on top.

This sausage stuffing can be prepared ahead of time and refrigerated overnight.

The butcher backed up into the meat grinder and got a little behind in his work.

Noodles Romanoff

This is a dish from my ancient past. In the days when "Pasta-Roni" and pasta side dishes in a box first came out. Noodles Romanoff was one of my favorites. But then, for some unknown reason, they stopped making it, and for 25 years I went into Romanoff withdrawals. But recently, I came on this recipe, by others who had the same longings as I did, that is easy to make and allows me to have my Romanoff fix whenever I'm in the mood.

Ingredients:

- 6 ounces of store bought egg noodles
- ½ cup of Sour Cream
- ¼ cup of Kraft® Macaroni & Cheese Powder (or other brand)
- ½ - 1 teaspoon minced garlic or ¼ - ½ teaspoon of garlic powder (to taste)
- ¼ teaspoon onion powder
- 2 tablespoon butter
- 1 tablespoon chopped chives (optional)

Directions:

Boil the noodles in salted water until done to desired wellness. Drain the noodles and return them to the same pot they were cooked in. This makes for less to clean up later.

While the noodles are still hot, add the butter and mix until the butter is entirely melted and all the noodles are coated. Add the Macaroni & Cheese Powder and stir until well mixed and all the noodles are coated, then add in all the other ingredients at once and mix until homogeneous. Serve at once.

Serves 4.

Some people like a dash of pepper also. If you go this route, use the fine ground pepper instead of the fresh ground, which sometimes comes too course.

If you don't finish this entire dish, you can keep it in the fridge and reheat it later over the stove or in the microwave by adding a small amount of milk and stirring frequently.

Noodles Romanoff

There was once a great czar in Russia named Rudolph the Red. He stood looking out the windows of is palace one day while his wife, the Czarina Katerina, sat nearby knitting. He turned to her and said, "Look my dear, it has begun to rain!" Without even looking up from her knitting she replied, "It's too cold to rain. It must be sleeting."

The Czar shook his head and said, "I am the Czar of all the Russias, and Rudolph the Red knows rain, dear!

Spinach with Shrimp

This is just a side to add a little flair to your meal, or maybe to impress guests.

Ingredients

- 1 tablespoon olive oil
- ¼ cup lemon juice
- ¼ cup olive oil
- 4 cloves garlic, minced
- ¼ teaspoon coarse black pepper
- ¼ teaspoon salt
- 2 teaspoons lemon zest
- 1 pound, any size, peeled and deveined
- 1 (6 ounce) bag spinach leaves (I use baby spinach leaves)

Preparation

Stir together garlic, pepper, salt and lemon zest. Blend in lemon juice and olive oil and set aside.

If you use large or jumbo shrimp, cut the shrimp into bite-sized pieces. Smaller shrimp may be used whole.

Heat 1 tablespoon of olive oil in a skillet over medium-high heat. Add the shrimp, and cook for 2 minutes.

Stir in the spinach and cook just until the greens are wilted and shrimp turn pink (about 2-3 minutes).

Stir in the lemon-olive oil mixture. Toss well.

Serve immediately.

Did you hear about the new restaurant on the moon? Great food, but no atmosphere.

Peppers and Mushrooms

This is a basic simple side that I think goes great with grilled lamb (see recipe).

Ingredients:

- 4 ounces of medium sized button mushrooms
- 1 large green pepper
- 2 tbls olive oil
- 2 tbls butter
- Salt
- A splash of dry white wine
- Fresh ground pepper
- Fresh or dried parsley

Preparation:

Slice the mushrooms into halves or quarters if they are too large. Clean and slice the pepper into long strips about ½ inch wide.

Put a skillet over medium-high heat and add the butter and oil. When the butter is melted and starts to bubble add the peppers and stir-fry them for about 1 minute. Add the mushroom pieces and sprinkle with about ¼ teaspoon of salt; stir-fry the contents until the peppers just start to soften. Add a splash of wine (to taste) and continue to stir until most of the wine has reduced. Salt and pepper to taste and sprinkle with fresh or dried parsley. Serve at once.

A bent-over old lady hobbled into a doctor's office.

Within minutes, she came out again but miraculously, she was standing up as straight as could be.

A man in the waiting room who had been watching her said in amazement; "My goodness, what did the doctor do to you?"

The old lady replied, "He gave me a longer cane!"

Fettuccine with Four Cheeses

This is a different kind of pasta side.

Ingredients:

- ¼ cup butter
- ½ cup half-and-half
- ½ cup shredded Gruyère cheese
- ¼ cup grated Parmesan cheese
- ½ cup crumbled Gorgonzola cheese
- ½ cup shredded mozzarella cheese
- ½ teaspoon salt
- 1/8 teaspoon freshly ground pepper
- 1 clove garlic, finely chopped
- 8 ounces uncooked fettuccine
- 2 tablespoons olive oil
- 1 tablespoon finely chopped parsley

Directions:

In a 2-quart saucepan, heat the butter and half-and-half over low heat until the butter has melted. Stir in the Gruyère cheese, Parmesan cheese, salt, pepper and garlic. Cook for 5 minutes, stirring occasionally.

Cook the fettuccine according to the package directions except add oil to the boiling water; drain.

Add the hot fettuccine to the sauce; add the Gorgonzola and mozzarella cheeses and toss using two forks. Sprinkle with the parsley and serve.

A Duck Walks Into A Store And Say's "I'd Like Some Lip Gloss!"

The Clerk Say's "Will That Be Cash Or Charge?"

The Duck Say's "Just Put It On My Bill!"

Garlic Asparagus

A fast and easy way to enjoy asparagus as a side that will go with almost any main course.

Ingredients:

- 1 or 2 bunches fresh asparagus
- 1 tablespoon butter
- 2 tablespoon olive oil
- 4 or 5 cloves garlic, minced

Directions:

Wash and trim the asparagus (I use the snapping method which has always worked perfectly for me) and discard the woody stems.

Fill a large skillet (12" or larger) with water to about 1 inch deep and heat to just about the boiling point. Blanch the asparagus until it turns a bright green (no more than a minute). Remove the asparagus and place immediately in cold water to stop the cooking. Discard the hot water, dry out the skillet and place back on the stove. Pat dry the asparagus.

Add the butter and oil to the skillet and heat under medium heat until the butter has melted and mixes with the oil. Add the garlic and stir to heat for about 30 seconds. Roll in the asparagus into the skillet and cook, constantly rolling and rotating the asparagus through the garlic mixture to coat all the stalks evenly until they are tender but still firm.

Serve immediately pouring remaining garlic oil over the plated asparagus.

Jonathan asked his young son, "Greg, do you think I'm a bad father?"
"My name is Andrew," replied his son.

Stir Fried Broccoli

This is a great alternative to boiled or steamed broccoli. Bet you never thought of sugar.

Ingredients:

- 2 pounds of fresh broccoli
- 2 tablespoons peanut oil or vegetable oil
- 1 teaspoon salt
- ½ - 1 teaspoon sugar
- 2 tablespoons chicken stock
- 1 teaspoon cornstarch dissolved in 1 tablespoon of chicken stock or water

Directions:

Wash the broccoli under cold water. Cut the flowerets from their stems in fairly large clusters and place in a bowl.

Peel the stems by cutting into the stringy skin and stripping it down like peeling an onion. Slice into 1-inch strips on the diagonal discarding the tough ends. Place these pieces in a separate bowl. Have the broccoli, sugar, salt, chicken stock and cornstarch mixture in easy reach.

Set a wok or large skillet over medium-high heat for 30 seconds. Add the oil and swish around to cover. Heat the oil for another 30 seconds. If the oil starts to smoke, lower the heat to medium. Add the broccoli <u>stems</u> and stir-fry for about 1 minute to coat all the broccoli with the oil.

Add the broccoli flowerets and stir-fry for 1 minute more.
Sprinkle the salt and sugar over the broccoli and then add the chicken stock and stir-fry to coat everything.

Cover the pan and cook over moderate heat for 2 to 3 minutes. The broccoli should be tender but still crisp.

Give the cornstarch a stir to recombine it and pour it into the pan. Stir until the broccoli is coated with a light, clear glaze. Serve at once.

There was once a cross-eyed teacher who couldn't control his pupils.

German Spaetzle

This is the other required part of a true Schnitzel dinner. These tiny dumplings are a variation on the everyday pasta sides that we are all used to. You will probably need a spaetzle maker to make the dumplings (they are inexpensive).

Ingredients:

- 3 cups all-purpose flour
- 1 cup milk
- 3 eggs
- 1/4 teaspoon ground nutmeg
- 1 pinch freshly ground white pepper
- 1/2 teaspoon salt
- 1 gallon hot water
- 2 tablespoons butter
- 2 tablespoons chopped fresh parsley

Directions:

Mix together flour, salt, white pepper, and nutmeg. In a separate bowl, beat the eggs well, and combine with the milk. Add the liquid to the dry ingredients a little at a time. Mix until smooth. The dough will be stiff and elastic. Let the dough rest for 10 to 15 minutes.

Bring a gallon of salted water to a boil in a large pot, and then reduce to a simmer. To form the spaetzle, press dough through a spaetzle maker or a large holed sieve or metal grater, directly into the simmering liquid. Do this in batches so you don't overcrowd the pot.

Cook for 3 to 4 minutes, stirring gently to prevent sticking. The spaetzle will float to the top when done. Use a slotted spoon to remove cooked spaetzle, drain well and put in a covered bowl. Repeat the process until al the dough is used.

Lightly butter and salt the spaetzle and sprinkle with parsley and serve in place of pasta, rice or potatoes.

If the spaetzle is too cool, melt some butter in a large skillet over medium heat and add the spaetzle; tossing to coat making sure they don't stick together. Cook the spaetzle for 1 to 2 minutes to give it some color, and then sprinkle with the chopped parsley and season with salt and pepper before serving. Alternately, microwave on high heat for about 30 seconds or when the desired temperature is reached.

New England Baked Beans

Again, New England roots. We always had canned baked beans while growing up, almost every Saturday night. Sometimes we fought for that random piece of pork fat that came with the beans, some call it the "Queen Bee", and sometimes we avoided it at all costs. This recipe allows you to add a more flavorful substitute, salt pork, which adds a nice flavor to the beans. You can freely substitute any kind of bacon for the salt pork, but remember that the flavor of the bacon will infuse in the beans. Be aware this is a 2-day recipe.

Ingredients:

- 1 pound dry navy or dry great northern beans
- 1/2 teaspoon salt
- 1/4 pound salt pork, diced (optional)
- 1 cup chopped onion
- 1/2 cup molasses
- 1/3 cup packed brown sugar
- 1 teaspoon dry mustard
- 1/2 teaspoon salt
- 1/8 teaspoon pepper

Directions:

The night before:

Rinse beans and pick over discarding unwanted beans. In a saucepan, bring the beans and 8 cups water to a boil; reduce heat. Simmer, covered for 1½ hours. Pour beans and liquid into a bowl; cover. Refrigerate overnight.

Next day:

Drain the beans, reserving 1 cup of liquid.
Place the beans in a Crock Pot. Add the 1 cup of reserved liquid.

Stir in the remaining ingredients. Cover and cook on low or high for 6 hours or until the beans are done. Stir before serving.

Serves 6 to 8.

Beer Biscuits

This is without doubt the simplest recipe in the world next to boiled water! These are very simple to make and simply wonderful tasting. The taste will depend on the type of beer used. A weak or light beer will not produce as flavorful a biscuit as a full-bodied beer will produce. Also, a dark beer will darken the dough and the end product will not be as attractive to the eye.

For those who don't have access to Bisquick, the Bisquick equivalent recipe is included.

Ingredients:

- 4 cups Bisquick or Bisquick equivalent*
- 3 tablespoons sugar
- 12 ounces beer (must be room temperature and standing)
- Melted butter to brush tops

Directions:

Preheat the over to 350° F.

Mix all the ingredients. The consistency will be a thick biscuit dough.

Fill well greased muffin tin, fill each cup to the top, or shape the dough in 1-1¼ inch high circular pieces like normal biscuits and place on a well greased cookie sheet.

Bake for 15 minutes.

Remove from oven and brush the tops with melted butter.

Return to oven and bake for another 5 minutes.

Serve hot.

*Bisquick Equivalent

- 5 cups flour
- 1/4 cup baking powder
- 2 Tbsp. sugar
- 1 teaspoon salt
- 1 cup Crisco (solid)

Mix together the flour, baking powder, sugar and salt. Cut in Crisco until mixture is crumbly. Store in an airtight container for up to 6 weeks or in the freezer for longer storage.

Makes approx: 6 cups

Beer Biscuits made in muffin tin

My stomach is flat.

The L is just silent

Quasimodo

Quasimodo, the famous Hunchback and bell ringer at the Cathedral of Notre Dame, sent word through the streets of Paris that he was going to retire and was looking for a new replacement bell ringer. Quasimodo decided that he would conduct the interviews personally.

One day, Quasimodo was in the belfry when he heard a knock at the door. When he answered the door, there stood an armless man, who announced that he wanted to apply for the bell ringer's job.

"But, you have no arms!" exclaimed Quasimodo

"Please, kind sir. Please let me at least show you I can do this. Besides, there are no other employers who will hire me and I am really desperate for a job."

Quasimodo listened and figured he give the man at least a chance and said, "See that huge bell over there? Lets see you ring it."

With that, the man reared back and made a dash for the bell, but tripped just before he reached the bell and his face smashed right into it pushing the bell well away and on its backswing hurtled the man over the railing and down 37 stories to the street below.

Quasimodo rushed down the stairs, as well as he could rush. When he reached the street, a crowd had gathered around the fallen figure. A gendarme turned to the hunchback and said, "Monsieur Quasimodo, who was this man?"

"I don't know his name," he sadly replied, "but his face sure rings a bell."

BUT, WAIT! WAIT! There's more ....

The next day, despite the unfortunate death of the armless campanologist, Quasimodo continued his interviews for the replacement bell ringer job. To his astonishment, the next applicant looked exactly like the first and also had no arms!

"I am the brother of the man who fell to his death from this very belfry. He knew nothing of bell ringing! I am the best bell ringer in our family. Please, allow me to demonstrate my skills."

The hunchback agreed to let the man try, but only after he agreed to ring the bells in the conventional way, by pulling the ropes. The man agreed and proceeded to ring the bells by leaping up and grabbing the ropes with his feet, but while pulling one of the ropes it broke, throwing the man over the railing and down the 37 stories to the street.

Again, Quasimodo descended to the street where a crowd had again gathered. As he approached the body, the same gendarme asked him who the man was. "I don't know his name," Quasimodo replied "but...he's a dead ringer for his brother."

DESSERTS

Whoopie Pies

*The girl quit her job at the doughnut factory because
she was fed up with the hole business.*

Basic Dessert Crepes

The only real difference between a normal crepe and a dessert crepe is the sugar.

Basic Dessert Crepe Recipe

Ingredients:

- 1 cup flour
- 1½ cups milk
- 2 eggs
- 1 tablespoon vegetable oil
- 2 tablespoons sugar
- 1/8 teaspoon salt

Directions:

There are several ways to make a crepe. The easiest is to use an electric crepe maker. Just follow the directions that come with the maker.

If you do not have one of those, then you can use a 10-inch skillet with a non-stick surface. Heat the skillet over medium heat. To test when the pan is hot enough, sprinkle a few drops of water on the surface. If the water sizzles and bounces, then the pan is ready.

Remove the pan from the heat and holding it with one hand, pour 2 tablespoons of the batter into the pan. Quickly start rotating the pan so that the batter coats the bottom in a thin even layer. Return the skillet to the heat and cook for 45 to 60 seconds.

When the crepe is lightly browned on the bottom, invert the pan and let the crepe drop onto a paper towel. You may need a small spatula to get the crepe started off the pan. Let each crepe cool.

Note that you do not have to cook the crepes on both sides. Just put the filling desired on the un-browned side and roll the crepe as desired exposing the browned side.

Stack cooled crepes between two layers of waxed paper. Use right away or freeze for up to several weeks before using.

Below I have provided 2 additional basic crepe batter recipes for dessert crepes to experiment with. Use fruits, cream, cheese or whatever you desire.

Chocolate Dessert Crepes

Ingredients:

- 1 cup flour
- 1½ cups milk
- 2 eggs
- 1 tablespoon vegetable oil
- 1/3 cup pre-sweetened cocoa powder
- 1 teaspoon vanilla

Lemon or Orange Dessert Crepes

Ingredients:

- 1 cup flour
- 1½ cups milk
- 2 eggs
- 2 tablespoons vegetable oil
- 1 tablespoon sugar
- 1½ teaspoons grated lemon or orange zest

I took the job at a bakery...

Because I kneaded dough!

Strawberry Crepes

This is my favorite crepe recipe; that's why it's here!

Ingredients:

- ½ cup strawberry preserves
- 4 teaspoons orange liqueur
- 1 quart strawberries cut in ¼ inch slices
- 6 whole strawberries for garnish
- 1½ cups of whipping cream
- 1 teaspoon vanilla
- 4 tablespoons confectioners sugar whipped into soft peaks
- 6 basic dessert crepes (see recipe)
- Sprinkle of confectioners sugar

Directions:

Mix the preserves with the liqueur. Pour the cream, 2 tablespoons of sugar and vanilla into a cold bowl and whip until whipped into soft peaks. Coat each crepe with about 1 tablespoon of the preserve mixture followed by an equal amount of the whipped cream centered in the crepe. Arrange an equal amount of the sliced strawberries on cream in each. Fold each end of the crepe over to form the crepe cylinder and rotate so that the folds are on the bottom of the plate. Place one of the whole strawberries on each plate and dust with powdered sugar, if desired. Chill in the refrigerator if desired. Serves 6.

Variation:

Strawberry Crepe Stacks

Use 10 basic dessert crepes instead of the 8 above.

Place one crepe, browned side down on a serving plate. Spread about 1 tablespoon of the preserve mixture. Next, spread about ¼ cup of the whipped cream and top with about ¼ cup of the sliced strawberries. Repeat this layering with the crepes browned side up 3 more times. Repeat to make a 2nd stack. Top each stack with a crepe, browned side up, and center 3 of the whole strawberries. Add any remaining cream around the edges and lightly dust with the powdered sugar. Chill in the refrigerator if desired. Slice into the desired number of slices and serve.

Strawberry Crepe Dessert

I have a fear of speed bumps...

But I'm slowly getting over it.

Whoopie Pies

There are several recipes for Whoopie Pies out there, but I find this one gives the best chocolate flavor and texture to the cake part.

Ingredients:

For the cakes:
- ½ cup unsweetened cocoa powder
- ½ cup whole milk
- 1 stick of unsalted butter, cut into 1 tablespoon pieces
- 1 cup sugar
- 1 teaspoon light corn syrup
- 2 large eggs, beaten
- 1½ cups flour
- 1 teaspoon baking powder
- 1 teaspoon baking soda
- ¼ teaspoon salt

Filling:

- 6 tablespoons of unsalted butter, softened
- ¾ cups confectioners' sugar
- ¾ cup Marshmallow Fluff
- 1 teaspoons vanilla
- Pinch of salt

Directions:

Preheat oven to 350° F.

Combine cocoa and milk in a medium saucepan and heat over low heat whisking to create a smooth paste. Add the butter, sugar and corn syrup and continue to whisk until the mixture is smooth and glossy and all the sugar has been dissolved. Set aside to cool.

Whisk the eggs into the cooled cocoa syrup until well blended.

Place the flour, baking powder, baking soda and salt into a mixing bowl. With the mixer on medium, slowly pour the cocoa syrup into the flour mixture until all the ingredients are well combined.

Drop about 1 tablespoon of the batter, or enough to make a 2 inch round pie, onto a well-greased cookie sheet or parchment paper about 3 inches apart. The batter will spread, so plan accordingly. Bake until top springs back up when touched, about 5 – 7 minutes. Remove to wire rack to cool.

For the filling, combine all the ingredients and beat with a mixer at medium speed until fluffy, about 2 minutes.

Spread the filling between two cakes to make a sandwich. Do not use a lot of filling or the result will be too sweet. Wrap each individual sandwich with plastic wrap to keep fresh.

Makes about a dozen 3-inch diameter pies.

Whoppie Pies wrapped for freshness

Sticks float. They would.

(If you don't get it, pretend Tonto is saying it!)

Pizzelle

You must have a pizzelle maker to make pizzelles. A pizzelle maker is like a small waffle iron that has designs on both upper and lower hot plates. Pizzelles are good plain, with a topping, or as the sandwich part of an ice cream sandwich.

Ingredients:

- 6 eggs
- 3½ cups flour, sifted
- 1½ cups sugar
- 1 cup margarine and butter (half each) melted
- 4 teaspoons baking powder
- 2 tablespoons vanilla

Directions:

Beat the eggs, adding sugar gradually. Beat until smooth. Add the melted margarine and butter, vanilla, sifted lour, baking powder to the egg mixture. Combine until it forms a dough sticky enough to be dropped by a spoon.

Place a heaping tablespoons worth of dough (you will determine how much after the first few are made) in the center of each form on the pizzelle maker, close and cook until golden.

Let cool and then place a large quantity in plastic bags for storage.

A man rushed into the doctor's office and shouted, "Doctor! I think I'm shrinking!"
The doctor calmly responded, "Now, settle down. You'll just have to be a little patient."

Ricotta Pie

Note … **this recipe is for making 2 pies**. This is because the Ricotta cheese around here comes in a large and small container. The large is too large for a single pie and the small is too small for a single pie. Cut recipe in half for a single pie.

Crust (for 2 pies)

- 2½ cups flour
- 8 egg yokes
- ½ teaspoon baking powder
- ½ cup sugar
- 1 teaspoon vanilla
- 1½ sticks butter

Directions:

Sift flour, sugar and baking powder. Crumble butter with fingers. Add the egg yolks and vanilla. Knead until smooth and uniform (add few drops of water if necessary). Roll between waxed paper to pie plate size. Make a pie shell in the pie plate with the crust. Each pie will be open topped.

Filling

- 1 Large container of Ricotta (3 pounds)
- 1 pound box of confectioner's sugar
- 8 egg whites
- 1 teaspoon flour
- 1 teaspoon vanilla

Directions:

Mix all the ingredients well, except the egg whites. In a separate bowl, beat whites well. Fold in whites with the other mixed ingredients thoroughly. Pour into crust. Sprinkle with cinnamon. Bake at 350° F for 35 to 40 minutes.

I was going to buy a book on phobias, but I was afraid it wouldn't help me.

Struffoli

Struffoli is an Italian "pick food". Arrange them stacked on a plate and as people walk by they will eat a few each time they walk by. Soon it will be noticed that these people are just walking around to pass by the plate.

Ingredients:

- 6 large eggs
- 1 stick (¼ pound) butter, softened
- ¼ cup sugar plus 2 tablespoons
- 3 cups all-purpose flour
- 1 scant teaspoon baking powder
- 1 teaspoon vanilla
- 1 cup honey
- Vegetable oil for deep-frying
- Colored sprinkles

Directions:

Whisk together eggs, butter, vanilla and the sugar. Whisk until frothy. Stir in baking powder, and then stir in flour. When well combined, work the mixture into a soft dough with your hands.

When nicely dough-like, divide into 4 pieces. Lightly flour a work surface, and roll each of the four pieces into a rope about the width of an index finger and a foot long. Cut the ropes into 1" pieces. Roll each piece into a small ball between the palms of your hands.

Heat oil to 375° F in a deep fryer. Cook small batches of 6-10 so you don't lower the frying oil temperature, fry the struffoli until they are golden brown.

Transfer with a slotted spoon to a paper towel to drain. Let excess oil drip back into fryer before putting struffoli on paper towels.

Combine the honey and 2 tablespoons of sugar in a large saucepan over low heat. Stir constantly until sugar dissolves into the honey. Turn heat to very low, just enough to keep warm. Add the drained struffoli, a few at a time, and turn them with a wooden spoon to coat on all sides.

Transfer struffoli to a large platter and mound them into a pyramid, shaping with wet hands. Sprinkle with the colored sprinkles and let stand for 1 to 2 hours. They will adhere to each other, but that's part of the fun - break off pieces with hands to eat. Long live struffoli!

Struffoli – the finished product!

King Ozymndias of Assyria was running low on cash after years of war with the Hittites. His last great possession was the Star of the Euphrates, the most valuable diamond in the ancient world.

Desperate, he went to Crosus, the pawn broker, to get a loan.

Crosus said, "I'll give you 100,000 dinars for it."

*"But I paid a million dinars for it," the king protested.
"Don't you know who I am? I am the king!"*

Crosus replied, "When you wish to pawn a Star, makes no difference who you are."

Mom's Blueberry Pie

My mother was a master pie maker. She would amaze everyone on how fast she could turn out pies … and all the crusts were perfect every time. The only difference is she always made her own crusts, which she had down to a fine art.

Ingredients:

- 4 cups fresh blueberries
- 2/3 cup sugar
- 7 tablespoons cornstarch
- 3 tablespoons water
- 2 tablespoons lemon juice
- 1 teaspoon cinnamon
- ¼ teaspoon allspice (optional)
- ¼ teaspoon nutmeg (optional)
- 2 tablespoons butter
- Pre-made piecrust

Crumb topping (if preferred):

- ¼ cup sugar
- ½ cup flour
- ¼ cup butter

Directions:

Preheat the over for 375° F.

Put the bottom half of the piecrust into a 9-inch pie dish, spread uniformly. Wash the blueberries. Rinse them in a colander or sieve in cold water and remove any leaves and pick off any stems left.

Combine the 2/3 cup sugar, cornstarch, and spices in a bowl and mix well. Add the lemon juice, and water and mix well. The result will be very thick, so don't worry.

Pour the blueberries to the piecrust and spread evenly. It is alright if the berries form a mound high above the pie lip. The berries will cook down.

Pour the sugar mixture over the blueberries as evenly as possible. It is not necessary to cover everything, just do as much as you can do as evenly as possible.

If you want the crumb topping, mix well the ingredients for the topping (above) and sprinkle the mixture over the top of the pie.

If you want a standard dough topping, then place a second piece of piecrust dough over the pie. Seal it against the edges with the piecrust holding the berries. Make decorative slits with a knife to allow steam to escape while cooking.

Bake at 375 for 1 hour.

Struffoli and Blueberry Pie

I thought I saw my eye doctor on an Alaskan island,
but it turned out to be an optical Aleutian.

Booze Cake

This was a favorite for office parties, since you could not bring alcohol into the office.

Ingredients:

- 1 package of Orange Supreme Cake Mix*
- 1 package vanilla instant pudding
- ½ cup vegetable oil
- 4 eggs
- ½ cup Orange juice

and either

- ¼ cup Galliano liqueur
- ¾ cup Vodka

or

- 1 cup Whiskey

Directions:

Preheat oven to 350° F. Mix all ingredients thoroughly and pour into well-greased tube pan. Bake for 50 minutes or until toothpick or probe comes out clean. Let cool and serve. May be topped with orange icing (see below).

Orange Icing

Ingredients:

- 1 cup powdered sugar
- 1½ to 2 tablespoons fresh orange juice
- 1 teaspoon Orange zest

Directions:

Wisk all ingredients until well mixed. Icing should be firm yet fluid. Drizzle over top of cake.

- Groceries don't have this cake mix on hand much any more, but it is available on-line.

I tried cooking supper with wine tonight, but it didn't go so well. After 5 glasses I forgot why I was even in the kitchen.

Zappole

This is an Italian fritter favorite and shows up at all the Italian holidays.

Ingredients:

- 2 cups flour
- 2 eggs
- 2 teaspoons baking powder
- ½ teaspoon salt
- 2 tablespoons of oil
- 1 cup milk
- Honey or confectioners sugar for coating

Directions:

In a deep fryer or deep skillet, heat 2 inches of vegetable oil to 375° F. Set a large wire rack over a baking sheet, top with paper towels and position near the cooking area.

In a large bowl, mix all ingredients. Mixture should be as thin as cake batter.

Drop one large tablespoon of batter in deep fryer and cook until golden. Remove with slotted spoon and place on rack to cool. Once cool, place on a large platter.

Sprinkle cooled zappoles with either powdered sugar or, even better, drizzle with honey to taste. Some like to keep them dry and dip each zappole into a bowl of honey.

No matter how much you push the envelope, it will still be stationery.

Magic (Meringue) Mushrooms

Ingredients:

- ½ cup egg whites (about 4 eggs)
- ¼ teaspoon cream of tartar
- ¼ teaspoon salt
- 1 teaspoon vanilla extract
- 1 cup white sugar
- 1 tablespoon unsweetened cocoa powder
- ¼ Cup Chocolate Chips

Directions:

Preheat the oven to 225° F. Line 2 cookie sheets with parchment paper.

Place room temperature egg whites in the bowl of an electric mixer fitted with a whisk attachment if you have one. Begin beating the egg whites on medium speed. Once they are very frothy, stop and add the cream of tartar. Start mixing again and continue to beat the egg whites until they form soft peaks. Increase the speed to high and gradually add the sugar, a tablespoon at a time. Beat the whites until they are very shiny and hold stiff peaks.

Place the meringue in a large zip-lock bag and push the mixture toward one corner, folding the other corner over, then twisting, allowing you to control the meringue. Cut off just the very tip of the exposed corner so the meringue can exit the bag. Then try it out by dotting four small beads of meringue at the corners of a cookie sheet. Set a sheet of parchment paper over the top; the meringue beads will provide a bond.

Make the mushroom caps by holding the bag over the parchment paper and push until a 1-inch mound of meringue forms. Wet the tip of your finger with water and gently round off any peaks to make a smooth surface.

For mushroom stems, form peaks on smaller mounds of meringue by pulling the bag up and away from the surface as you push.

Bake for 1 hour in the preheated oven, or until the caps are dry enough to easily remove from the cookie sheets. Set aside to cool completely.

To construct "mushrooms":

Melt the chocolate chips in a microwave-safe dish in the microwave for about one minute or until melted. Make a hole smaller than a pea in the bottom of a mushroom cap with a toothpick or skewer. Dip the tip of the stem in the melted chocolate and press into the hole in the cap. Allow the chocolate "glue" to harden (it only takes a minute). Place the mushroom upright on its stem and dust the cap lightly with cocoa powder.

This mushroom walks into a bar and starts hitting on this woman. She, of course, turns him down. Not willing, to give up, he pleads with her, "C'mon lady, I'm a fun guy."

Two Eskimos sitting in a kayak were chilly; but when they lit a fire in the craft, it sank, proving that you can't have your kayak and heat it too.

SAUCES AND DIPS

Jaeger Schnitzel (Spaetzle) Sauce

My Spaghetti Gravy

I refuse to get into that argument over whether you call it gravy or sauce. It's gravy!! This is MY recipe and I'll call it what I want!

Everyone loves my spaghetti gravy, or so I'm told, but the first thing you have to understand is that this recipe is not an exact thing. I make my gravy "by feel" as far as measurements are concerned. I will provide the basics, but you have to make it as you feel the day you make it. It comes out better that way.

Ingredients:

- 4 cans (28-ounce size) Italian style crushed tomatoes
- 2 cans (6-ounce size) tomato paste
- 6 tablespoons Olive Oil
- 1 large sweet or yellow onion
- 3 tablespoon of minced garlic or to taste
- 1 cup red wine, I like Burgundy or other good drinking wine
- 2 tablespoons of sugar
- Fresh (finely chopped) or dried basil
- Fresh (finely chopped) or dried oregano
- Italian seasoning
- Salt
- Pepper

Optional: Sausages, meatballs, green peppers, chicken parts, steak

Directions:

Take the onion and cut into desired sized slices or chop if desired.

Put the olive oil in a 6-8 quart stockpot and heat under medium high heat. Once hot add the onion and cook until the onions become soft. Lower the heat to medium and add the garlic. Stir with the onions for about 1 minute. Add the canned tomatoes, tomato paste, wine, sugar, about ½ teaspoon of salt and ¼ teaspoon of pepper and mix well.

Lower the heat to simmer. Now start adding the seasoning. This is done to taste. I usually start with about 1 tablespoon each of the Italian seasoning, basil and oregano and work up from there, adding more salt and pepper if needed. It is important that after you add the first batch of seasoning that you mix them well and let them cook for about 15 minutes before tasting the gravy and adding more. Repeat as needed until you are happy with the result. At this point you can add the optional meats (see below for details).

Cover the stockpot and let the gravy simmer for at least 2 hours, stirring occasionally. Turn off the heat and let sit covered until room temperature and then put in the refrigerator. The gravy will keep for up to two weeks, if it lasts that long. Just reheat as needed. You may also freeze it for later use.

Optional Items:

When using the optional ingredients, make sure you understand that the flavor of the item you use will permeate the gravy even after the items are gone. If you use sausages, the gravy will have a distinct sausage flavor. If you use hot sausages, the gravy will have a hot sausage flavor. All these extras are added when you start the simmer process.

Sausages or meatballs:

Use Italian sausages, either sweet or mild (but use what you want), and place them, uncooked, in the gravy. You can put in as many as can fit in the stockpot as long as all the sausages are totally covered by the gravy. The simmer time should be increased to 3 to 4 hours. Stir the sausages or meatballs several times during cooking.

Green Peppers:

Cut the peppers into 1 inch slices or cubes. Add them into the stockpot at the same time as the onions. Follow the rest of the directions as stated.

Chicken:

Broil, grill, pan fry or bake seasoned chicken pieces until about half cooked. The chicken does not have to be cooked through. Add the pieces to the gravy at the simmer stage and cook as usual. The simmer time should be increased to 4 hours depending on the thickness of the chicken pieces.

Steak:

Broil or grill a seasoned sirloin or flank steak to rare. Cut into slices against the grain to the thickness and length desired. Add to the gravy at the simmer stage. Also see recipe for Braciole in the main courses section.

This grasshopper walks into a bar, and the bartender says "Hey! We have a drink named after you!" The grasshopper replies "Really? You have a drink named Steve?!"

Simple Marinara Sauce

This recipe makes a less intense and thicker sauce than the gravy recipe above. That makes is nice to use as a dip or spread because it is not overpowering.

Ingredients:

- 1 can (28-ounce size) Italian crushed tomatoes
- 2 tablespoons extra virgin olive oil
- 4 medium garlic cloves, minced
- 1 can (6-ounce size) tomato paste
- 1¼ teaspoon oregano (or more, to taste)
- ¼ teaspoon salt
- ¼ teaspoon pepper
- 1/3 cup fresh parsley, chopped
- 3 tablespoons red wine

Directions:

Heat the oil in a medium saucepan over medium high heat; add the garlic. Sauté for 15 seconds, being careful not to let the garlic burn. Add the tomatoes, oregano, salt, pepper, and wine. Bring sauce to a boil, reduce heat, and simmer for 20 minutes. Remove from heat and stir in parsley. Can be used right away or refrigerated.

A ship carrying blue paint collided with a ship carrying red paint.
The crew is believed to be marooned.

Balsamic Barbeque Sauce

This sauce is great for chicken or steak.

Ingredients:

- 1 cup balsamic vinegar
- ¾ cup ketchup
- 1/3 cup brown sugar
- 1 garlic clove, minced
- 1 tablespoon Worcestershire sauce
- 1 tablespoon Dijon mustard
- ½ teaspoon salt
- ½ teaspoon freshly ground black pepper

Preparations:

Combine all the ingredients in a small saucepan and stir until all the ingredients are incorporated and the mixture is smooth. Simmer over medium heat until reduced by 1/3, about 15 to 20 minutes.

For the chicken or steak:

Preheat a gas or charcoal grill. Season the meat with salt and pepper. Lightly coat with some of the barbeque sauce using a pastry brush and place on the grill. Place the remaining barbeque sauce, still in the small saucepan, over low heat or on the edge of a grill and allow to gently simmer while the meat cooks.

Cook the chicken about 8 minutes per side. Cook the steaks starting at about 4 to 6 minutes per side depending if you want medium rare or medium. Brush the meat with barbeque sauce every few minutes. Remove the meat from the grill and let rest for at least 5 minutes. Serve with the heated barbeque sauce alongside.

A boiled egg is hard to beat.

Subway's Sweet Onion Chicken Teriyake Sauce

Every once in a while, fast food restaurants come up with something new that is really good. Such is the case with Subway's Sweet Onion Chicken Teriyaki sandwich. The sauce is what makes it so good and here is a close clone.

Ingredients:

- ½ cup light corn syrup
- 1 Tablespoon minced white onion
- 1 Tablespoon red wine vinegar
- 2 teaspoons white distilled vinegar
- 1 teaspoon balsamic vinegar
- 1 teaspoon brown sugar
- 1 teaspoon dry buttermilk
- ¼ teaspoon lemon juice
- 1/8 teaspoon poppy seed
- 1/8 teaspoon salt
- 1 pinch cracked black pepper
- 1 pinch garlic powder

Directions:

Combine all ingredients in a small microwave-safe bowl.

Heat mixture uncovered in the microwave for 1 to 1 1/2 minutes on high until mixture boils rapidly.

Whisk well, cover and cool.

Use this as intended in a sandwich or can even be used as a salad dressing.

Why do French chickens only lay one egg at a time? Because one egg is un oeuf!

Lobster Sauce

As stated before, there is no lobster in lobster sauce. The name comes from the sauce that is used to prepare Lobster Cantonese. Nonetheless, this is a tasty sauce and worth the effort to make.

Ingredients:

- ¼ pound ground pork
- 2 teaspoons soy sauce
- 1 tablespoon fermented black beans
- 1 garlic clove
- 2 green onions (scallions)
- 1 tablespoon soy sauce
- 1 teaspoon granulated sugar
- ¾ cup chicken broth
- 2 tablespoons water
- 2 eggs, beaten
- ¼ teaspoon salt
- Pepper to taste
- 2 tablespoons oil for stir-frying
- 2 tablespoons cornstarch dissolved in 3 tablespoons water

Directions:

Add the last 2 tablespoons of oil to the pan and heat under high heat until it just starts to smoke; then lower the heat to medium high. Quickly add the black bean sauce and garlic and stir-fry for a few seconds to heat thoroughly being careful not to burn the garlic. Add the ground pork and stir-fry until the pork is no longer pink. Add the soy sauce, salt, pepper, sugar, scallions and stir to mix. At this point you can add shrimp, scallops, lobster or whatever main course planned. Add the chicken stock, cover and bring to a boil. Stir the cornstarch mixture to recombine and add it to the pan. Stir constantly until the sauce thickens, about 30 seconds, and then pour in the beaten eggs in a slow stream while lifting the sauce from the edges to merge with all the other ingredients without further cooking. Transfer to heated platter and serve at once.

"Once, during Prohibition, I was forced to live for days on nothing but food and water."
- W.C. Fields

Mornay Sauce

This is a classic Mornay Sauce recipe.

Ingredients:

- 3 tablespoons butter
- 3 tablespoons all-purpose flour
- ¼ teaspoon ground nutmeg
- ¾ teaspoon salt
- 1/8 teaspoon white pepper
- 1 cup light cream, half & half or milk, warmed
- ¼ cup dry white wine
- 1/3 cup shredded Swiss cheese or any desired cheese

Directions:

In a saucepan melt the butter. Add in the flour, nutmeg, salt and a dash of pepper and blend to make a roux. Add the cream all at once and cook until contents gets thick and bubbly. Stir in the wine. Add the cheese and stir until melted. Makes 1½ cups.

A man went to his dentist for a checkup, and the dentist saw that his dental plate was all corroded.

The dentist asked, "What have you been doing? Have you changed your diet or anything?"

The patient said, "I've discovered Hollandaise sauce and eat it every chance I get. Maybe that's what's causing the problem."

The dentist answered, "Oh, I see. In that case, I'll make you a new plate out of chrome."

The patient was puzzled. "Chrome? Why chrome?" he asked.

The dentist answered, "Because there's no plate like chrome for the Hollandaise."

Jaeger Schnitzel (Spaetzle) Sauce

This sauce also goes well on Spaetzle. If you are going to do pork schnitzel, use chicken broth instead of beef.

Ingredients

- 1 tablespoon butter
- ¼ cup minced shallot (or onion if you can't find shallots)
- 3 cups mushrooms
- 2½ cups beef broth
- ¼ cup flour
- ¼ teaspoon salt or to taste

Directions

Melt butter.

Sauté the shallots until clear.

Toss in mushrooms until mushrooms are sautéed.

Place flour in a separate bowl, slowly whisk in beef broth. Adding wet to dry helps prevent lumps.

Pour beef broth mixture into mushroom pan boil for 5-10 minutes until thickened; stir fairly often so it doesn't stick.

What do you call a hippie's wife?

Mississippi.

Cocktail Sauce

Why buy cocktail sauce in the store when it is so easy to make at home, plus you can make it as bland or spicy as you desire.

Ingredients:

- ½ cup ketchup
- ½ cup Chili Sauce
- 3 tablespoons prepared horseradish
- 2 teaspoons lemon juice
- ½ teaspoon Worcestershire Sauce
- ½ teaspoon hot sauce, optional

Directions:

Add all the ingredients into a bowl and mix until well blended. Adjust ingredients to suit your taste.

Makes 8 ounces.

Tips:

- Use the zest and juice of one whole lemon instead of just the juice
- Adjust the amount of horseradish you use as this is the major "hot" ingredient
- If you want to be daring, add ¼ cup of vodka to spike the sauce

What do you call a line of rabbits walking backwards?

A receding hairline

Rudy's Barbeque Sauce

I've been to Rudy's. Rudy's is a great barbeque place in Texas. They have their own barbeque sauce, which is terrific. This is a good clone to their sauce; it's close. This recipe yields about 2 cups and it keeps in the refrigerator a long time.

- 1 (8 ounces) can tomato sauce
- 1 cup ketchup
- ½ cup brown sugar
- 2 ½ tablespoon white vinegar
- 2 tablespoon Worcestershire sauce
- ¼ cup lemon juice (2 lemons)
- 1 teaspoon garlic powder
- 1 teaspoon coarse black pepper
- ¼ teaspoon cumin
- 1/8 teaspoon cayenne pepper

Combine all ingredients in a large pot. Simmer until slightly reduced

Marie Rose Sauce

My grandson, Elijah, who lives in England, loves this awesome sauce and taught me to love it, too. It's really simple and you can add whatever meets your fancy. Good in sandwiches, as salad dressing, on baked potatoes, Elijah's favorite Prawn Salad, and a thousand other things.

Ingredients:

- 3 tablespoons of Mayonnaise
- 1 tablespoon Ketchup
- A splash of Worcestershire Sauce (to taste)
- A splash of lemon juice (to taste)
- 1 tablespoon of Brandy (optional – not for the kids)

Directions:

Mix well and serve.

Chinese Spicy Dipping Sauce

Ingredients:

- 1/3 cup water
- 2 tablespoons soy sauce
- 2 tablespoons Hoisin sauce
- 2 tablespoons sake or dry Sherry
- ½ teaspoon sugar
- ½ teaspoon chili powder

Directions:

In a small saucepan, mix together all the ingredients Bring to a boil then reduce heat to simmer. Simmer uncovered for about 5 minutes until reduced to ½ cup. Serve warm or cool. Makes ½ cup.

Honey Dipping Sauce

Ingredients:

- ½ cup honey
- 2 tablespoons soy sauce
- ¼ teaspoon freshly ground pepper
- 1 teaspoon grated gingerroot

Directions:

In a small saucepan, mix together all the ingredients Cook until warm throughout. Serve warm. Makes 2/3 cup.

If the cops arrest a mime, do they tell him he has the right to remain silent?

Plum Sweet and Sour Sauce

I seldom use the pineapple in this recipe, but it is here if you want it.

Ingredients:

- 1 (20-ounce) can crushed pineapple in heavy syrup (optional)
- 1 cup sugar
- 1 cup water
- 1 cup vinegar
- 1 tablespoon soy sauce
- 2 tablespoon cornstarch
- 2 tablespoon cold water
- 1 cup plum sauce

Directions:

Heat pineapple with syrup (if using), sugar, water, vinegar, and soy sauce to boiling. Mix cornstarch and 2 tablespoons water; stir into the mixture. Heat to boiling, stirring constantly. Cool to room temperature; stir in plum sauce. Cover and refrigerate. Makes 6 cups.

Sweet and Sour Dipping Sauce

Ingredients:

- ½ cup packed brown sugar
- 1 tablespoon cornstarch
- 1/3 cup chicken stock
- 1/3 cup red wine vinegar
- 1 tablespoon soy sauce
- 1 glove garlic, minced
- 1 teaspoon grated gingerroot

Directions:

In a small saucepan, mix together the sugar and cornstarch. Stir in the chicken stock, vinegar, soy sauce, garlic and gingerroot. Cook and stir over medium heat until thick and bubbly, then cook and stir for 2 minutes more. Serve warm. Makes ¾ cup.

Teriyaki Sauce

Quick and simple. This is slightly different than some of the teriyaki sauces used in other recipes in this book; others are more specific to the dish they are prepared with. Feel free to use whichever of the teriyaki recipes you like best.

Ingredients:
- ½ cup dark soy sauce
- ½ cup Mirin (sweetened sake)
- 1 tablespoon sugar or brown sugar

Optional:
- Grated or minced ginger
- Chopped scallions
- Minced garlic
- Honey
- Pineapple
- Orange juice
- Chopped Jalapeno Pepper or other mild chili

Directions:
Add all the ingredients into a saucepan and stir under low heat until all the sugar has been dissolved into the liquid. Sauce may be used right away or refrigerated for weeks.

Honey Mustard Dipping Sauce

Ingredients:

- 1/4 cup mayonnaise
- 2 tablespoons honey
- 1 tablespoon mustard
- 2 teaspoons Dijon mustard
- 2 teaspoons freshly squeezed lemon

Directions:

Combine all ingredients and mix until smooth.

<u>Lemon Dipping Sauce</u>

Need text here

Ingredients:

- ¼ Cup chicken broth
- 2 tablespoons lemon juice
- 2 tablespoons honey
- 1 tablespoon vinegar
- 1 tablespoon vegetable oil
- 1 ½ teaspoons catsup
- ¼ teaspoon garlic salt
- 1 teaspoon cornstarch
- 1 teaspoon cold water

Directions:

Mix the first seven ingredients in a 1-quart saucepan. Separately, mix the cornstarch and cold water then stir it into the broth mixture. Heat until boiling stirring constantly. The sauce will thicken. Cover and refrigerate until ready to use. Serve at room temperature.

People who tell really bad puns shouldn't just be banished,
they should be drawn and quoted.

Ricotta-Tomato Dip

Ingredients:

- 2 cups tomato sauce
- 1 cup ricotta cheese
- Basil (for garnish)
- Olive oil

Directions:

Simmer the tomato sauce in a small skillet. Add the ricotta in small dollops and warm through. Garnish with basil and drizzle with olive oil.

Pizza Dip

Ingredients:

- 1 cup ricotta cheese
- 1 cup Italian tomato sauce
- ½ cup shredded mozzarella cheese
- ½ cup chopped pepperoni

Directions:

Preheat oven to 375° F.

In a 9-inch pie plate, evenly layer the ricotta cheese. Top with ¼ cup of the pepperoni and ½ cup of mozzarella. Carefully spread the sauce over the cheese. Sprinkle the remaining mozzarella and pepperoni over the top.

Bake for 15 minutes or until it is hot. Remove and let stand for 10 minutes.

Serve with garlic bread or crackers for dipping.

You may substitute any of the following for the pepperoni: sliced pitted olives, sliced mushrooms, chopped sweet peppers, chopped onions, chopped or ground Italian sausage.

Clam Dip

Ingredients:

- 2 - 6 ½ ounce can of minced or chopped clams
- 1 - 12 ounce container of whipped cream cheese
- 1 tablespoon Worcestershire Sauce
- ½ teaspoon garlic powder
- ½ teaspoon onion powder

Directions:

Drain the clam juice out of the clams and reserve. Put the cream cheese in an oversized bowl; add the drained clams and Worcestershire sauce, garlic powder, onion powder and mix well. If the dip is too thick, add some clam juice and/or Worcestershire a little at a time until it is the desired consistency. Add more onion and garlic powder to taste.

Serve with cold vegetables, chips or crackers for dipping.

I was doing an overnight at a hotel away from home. And I took my computer down to the bar to do some data entries. I sat down at the bar and I asked the bartender "What's the wifi password?"

Bartender: "You need to buy a drink first".

Me: Okay, I'll have a beer.

Bartender: We have Molsons Canadian on tap.

Me: Sure. How much is that?

Bartender: $8.00.

Me: Ok. Here you are. What's the wifi password?

Bartender: youneedtobuyadrinkfirst, no spaces and all lowercase.....

SOUPS, STEWS AND STOCKS

Lamb Stew

"Soup is just a way of screwing you out of a meal."
- Jay Leno

Wes's World Famous New England Clam Chowder

Everyone who has tried this clam chowder loves it. They love it in New England. They love it in Florida. They love it in Texas. They even love it in the U.K. I especially love the great taste the salt pork adds. **This recipe is for making a full 6 quarts of chowder**. That is because when I make it, everyone around wants some. Adjust the recipe if you don't want to feed the neighborhood.

Ingredients:

- 4 pounds potatoes, peeled and cut into ¾ inch dice
- 1 large 51-ounce can chopped clams
- 8 to 12 ounces Salt pork, thinly sliced and cut into ½ inch strips
- 3 stalks celery, cut into 1/3 inch dice
- 2 medium yellow onions cut into ¾ inch dice
- 6 tablespoons butter
- 2 large dried bay leaves
- 2 tablespoon thyme
- 4 cloves garlic, minced
- ¼ cup freshly chopped Italian parsley
- 4 cups of heavy cream or half –and-half
- 4 cups clam broth (from can of clams, store bought or home made)
- Salt
- Pepper

Place a large pot or Dutch oven over medium-low heat. Add the salt pork and cook, stirring frequently until it starts to get crispy. Do not over cook. Add the 4 tablespoons of butter, onions, garlic, celery, thyme and bay leaves and sauté until the onions are softened but not brown.

Add the potatoes and 4 cups of clam broth. There should be just enough liquid to barely cover the potatoes. If not, add more broth or water. Cover the pot, turn the heat to high and let boil for about 10 minutes or until the potatoes are soft on the outside, but still firm.

Remove the pot from the heat and stir in the cream, parsley and clams. Season with salt and pepper to taste and add the remaining 2 tablespoons of butter. Cover and let cure for at least an hour, I recommend at least 3 hours.

New England Clam Chowder

To serve, heat over low heat until chowder is hot throughout (do not let it boil). Place desired chowder in a bowl, sprinkle with parsley and add a pat of butter if desired. Serve with Saltine or Oyster crackers.

Serves about 12 as a main course and a ton of people as an appetizer.

If you like your chowder thick, do the following just before you reheat the chowder. Make a roux consisting of the 2 tablespoons of bacon fat and 2 tablespoons butter (or just 4 tablespoons of butter) and 4 tablespoons of flour.

Add butter and bacon fat in a medium skillet and heat to melt the butter until hot, but NOT smoking. Add the flour and mix well; the flour will bubble. Mix well until homogeneous. With a ladle, add some of the chowder liquid and continue stirring to thin out the roux. Add as much liquid as you feel needed. Then add the entire contents to the chowder and stir until all the roux is completely dissolved in the chowder. Stir often during the reheating process.

How does Moses make his tea? Hebrews it.

Calamari Stew with Garlic Toast

This is a different seafood stew with a little kick to it. Makes a great cold weather meal.

Ingredients:

For the Calamari Stew:

- 2 tablespoons olive oil
- 2 cloves garlic, cut in half
- 1½ cups tomato sauce
- 1 cup white wine
- 1 teaspoon fresh chopped thyme leaves
- ¼ teaspoon red pepper flakes (or to taste)
- ½ teaspoon salt
- ¼ teaspoon freshly ground black pepper
- 1 pound calamari (squid), bodies cleaned and thinly sliced and tentacles whole

For the Garlic Toast:

- 4 to 6 slices of bread
- Olive oil, for drizzling
- 2 to 3 whole cloves garlic

Directions:

For the Calamari Stew: Warm the olive oil over medium heat in a medium pot. Add the garlic and let cook until fragrant, about 2 minutes. Remove the garlic. Add the tomato sauce, white wine, thyme, red pepper flakes, salt, and pepper. Bring the mixture to a simmer. Add the calamari and stir to combine. Continue to cook until the mixture comes back up to a simmer, about 2 more minutes. Serve immediately with the Garlic Toasts.

For the Garlic Toast: Preheat the oven to 350° F.

Meanwhile, drizzle the bread slices with olive oil. Toast until the bread is crisp and turning golden brown, about 8 to 10 minutes. Remove from the oven and rub the top of the toasts with whole garlic cloves. Serve immediately with the Calamari Stew.

Serves 4.

Calamari Stew with Garlic Toast

I made a belt out of watches.

It was a waist of time.

Shrimp Chowder

A simple quick soup that you can use shrimp, crab or even,
if you want to be daring, lobster.

Ingredients:

- 3 tablespoons butter
- 1 small rib celery
- ¼ medium onion, peeled
- 1 small carrot, halved
- Pinch of marjoram
- Pinch of ground nutmeg
- 1 tablespoon lemon juice
- 2 cups chicken broth
- 8 ounces shrimp, or crab (or whatever you choose) cleaned, shelled and deveined
- 1 cup ½ & ½

Directions:

Place butter, celery, onion, carrot, marjoram, nutmeg, lemon juice, and chicken broth into a blender. Turn blender on and slowly increase speed to medium and blend for about 10 seconds to desired consistency.

Pour into a 4-quart saucepan and simmer for 10 minutes. Add shrimp and cook for 5 minutes or until shrimp is done (all pink). Add the milk and butter and continue to heat until chowder is hot, but not boiling. Serve immediately with oyster crackers or the like.

Shrimp Chowder

I don't suffer from insanity; I enjoy every minute of it.

Lamb Stew

Ingredients:

- 3 to 4 lbs leg of lamb, cut into 1 ½ " cube
- 2 tablespoons butter
- 1 tablespoon vegetable oil
- 2 cups water
- 1 cup chicken broth
- 1 to 2 teaspoon salt, or to taste
- ¼ teaspoon thyme, crushed
- ¼ teaspoon pepper
- 2 cloves garlic, mashed & minced
- 4 medium potatoes, quartered
- 8 small white onions, peeled or 1 large onion sliced
- 2 ribs celery, cut in ¼ inch pieces
- 3 small carrots, cut in 2-inch pieces
- 1 package frozen peas, (16 ounces)
- 8 ounces fresh mushrooms, sliced
- 1 cup milk
- 1/3 cup flour
- 2 tablespoons chopped parsley

Directions:

Over medium heat, brown lamb in the butter and oil in a large stockpot or Dutch oven. Add the water, broth, thyme, garlic, salt and pepper. Cover and simmer for 1 hour.

Remove any surface fat. Add the potatoes, carrots, celery and onion; simmer, covered, until vegetables are tender, about 15 to 20 minutes.

Add peas and simmer for 5 minutes. Combine milk and flour; stir until smooth. Add the milk mixture to simmering stew gradually and simmer for about 1 minute, or until thickened. Taste and adjust seasonings.

Serves 6.

Lamb Stew with dumplings

A small piece of rope climbed onto a barstool.

The bartender said he did not serve rope in his bar, and tossed it out to the street.

The rope asked a passerby to tie him into a knot, and then ruffle both ends.

The rope went back into the bar, the bartender looked down at him and said, "Hey aren't you that same piece of rope I just tossed out?"

The rope responded: "No sir, I am a frayed knot."

Shrimp Hot Pot Soup

I think this is the last shrimp recipe.

Ingredients:

- 4 cups shrimp stock
- 1/8 pound Angel Hair pasta broken into 2 inch pieces
- 3 scallions, white and greens, chopped
- 6-12 large shrimp, shelled and deveined
- 1/8 teaspoon Cayenne pepper, or to taste
- ¼ teaspoon salt

Optional:
- 1 stalk celery, thinly cut
- 3 medium mushrooms, sliced

Directions:

Cook the pasta in salted boiling water (not the stock) until almost done, then drain and add to a saucepan containing the stock, scallions, pepper, salt and shrimp (and optional ingredients if desired). Bring contents to a boil, lower the heat and simmer for 5 minutes. Adjust seasoning to taste. Serves 4-6.

Shrimp Hot Pot Soup

Chicken Noodle Soup

Nothing tastes better than good old homemade chicken soup. Why buy the canned stuff or stuff in a pouch when this is so simple to make? Besides, this uses real chicken.

Ingredients:

- ½ medium onion, thinly sliced
- 1 small carrot, thinly sliced
- 2 stalks celery, thinly sliced
- 2 sprigs fresh thyme
- 1 tablespoon whole flat-leaf parsley leaves
- 6 cups chicken stock
- ½ cup water
- Kosher salt and freshly ground black pepper
- 1/3 pound egg noodles (preferably wide ones)
- 1¼ cups sliced or shredded cooked chicken (meat from about one breast)

Put the onion, carrots, celery, thyme, parsley, chicken broth, and water in a medium pot; season with salt and pepper to taste. Bring to a simmer over medium high heat. Simmer until the vegetables are almost tender, about 5 minutes.

Cook the noodles in salted boiling water (not the stock) until almost done, then drain and add to a saucepan containing the stock.

Add the chicken, simmer for 5 minutes, and then adjust the seasoning if necessary with salt and pepper.

I used to run a dating agency for chickens...

But I was struggling to make hens meet!

Stocks

Stocks are always good to have on hand, whether for used to flavor main dishes or to make soups. Today you can readily buy chicken stock, beef stock and vegetable stock at your local store. But, why buy it when it is so easy and inexpensive to make. Don't throw away those shrimp shells or chicken parts. Make your own stock. Below are the common ingredients for most stocks.

Common Stock Ingredients:

- 1 fresh carrot, peeled and sliced
- 1 onion roughly cut up
- 1 stalk of celery sliced
- 1 bay leaf
- 1 teaspoon kosher salt
- 1 teaspoon thyme
- About 6 quarts of water

Shrimp Stock

Take the shells from 3 to 4 pounds of shrimp and ad them to a 7 quart stock pan. Add the water and bring to a boil. Remove from the heat and skim off any impurities that may rise to the surface. Put the pan back on the heat and add the rest of the common ingredients. Let boil for about 10 minutes and reduce heat to simmer. Cover and let simmer for 40 minutes. Remove from the heat and let steep for about 15 minutes. Immerse the pan in cold water, making sure no water gets into the stock, to cool down the stock. When cool, pour the stock through a fine mesh strainer or cheesecloth and throw away the solids. Refrigerate immediately. The stock should keep for a few weeks in the refrigerator, or, you can freeze it and it will keep for several months.

Chicken Stock

I usually save and freeze chicken parts (backs, gizzards, wing tips, giblets) until I have enough to make the stock. Usually the parts from two good sized chickens are enough for a good stock.

Take the unfrozen chicken parts and fry them with the onion in the stock pan until the chicken starts to brown and the onions turn translucent. Add the water and bring to a boil. Remove from the heat and skim off any impurities that may rise to the surface. Put the pan back on the heat and add the rest of the common ingredients. Let boil for about 10 minutes and reduce heat to simmer.

Cover and let simmer for 2 hours. Remove from the heat and let cool. When cool, pour the stock through a fine mesh strainer or cheesecloth and throw away the solids. Refrigerate immediately. The stock should keep for a few weeks in the refrigerator, or, you can freeze it and it will keep for several months.

Other Stocks

All stocks are prepared in a similar manner. You can make beef stock, veal stock, lamb stock, vegetable stock, shrimp stock, lobster stock, or any other stock that you might find the urge for doing.

Other Options

Grocery stores now carry many types of prepared stock such as chicken, beef and vegetable. These stocks come in convenient sizes and can be stored for long periods of time.

Bouillon may also be used in place of stock in any recipe. By using bouillon, there is less control over the seasonings and flavor in the recipe. But, if you are not too fussy and prefer the convenience of bouillon, by all means use it. Bouillon cubes are available in beef, chicken, vegetable, shrimp and others.

"Doctor, you've got to help me - I just can't stop my hands from shaking!"

"Do you drink a lot of coffee?"

"Not really – I spill most of it!"

Appendix

Stegosaurus Tail

The Stegosaurus Tail is a multi-purpose kitchen utensil that is used for both food preparation and child discipline.

For food preparation, the Stegosaurus Tail is used as a tool for handling long unruly pasta both during cooking and as a pasta server.

Domesticated Stegosaurus Tail

Stegosaurs Tail in the wild

The Stegosaurs Tail is most effectively used as a child intimidation and control device for the dinner table. It is used in three separate stages as follows:

Stage 1: When the child first is in need of discipline at the table, the alpha-parent should simply place the tail, spike side up, next to them within easy grasping distance, and then just look at the child in an intimidating manner. This usually will produce the desired results.

Stage 2: If Stage 1 fails, or starts to lose its effectiveness, the alpha-parent should grasp the tail firmly in one hand at the first sign of disorder and firmly slap the tail on the table, flat side down, with moderate to heavy force, depending on the situation. The resulting sharp noise will usually cause all within hearing distance, including neighbors within a 100-foot radius, to discontinue their current activities and focus on the alpha-parent. This should achieve the desired result, at which point you should return to Stage 1 operation.

Stage 3: If, for some reason beyond logic, Stage 2 does not achieve the desired result, the alpha-parent must resort to actually applying the Stegosaurus Tail to the back side of the chief antagonist's hand in a firm manner such as utilized in Stage 2, yet not so firm that bones actually may be broken, as tempting as this may be. The alpha-parent must show restraint. This result will always restore full control restored to the gathering. Normal conversation and/or the partaking and consumption of culinary delights may now continue as planned.

Note: If used properly, the alpha-parent need never speak a word during any of the three stages, although some like to add a little personal touch to its use. But as a general rule, all touches should be limited to Stage 3.

The Stegosaurus Tail has been in use for over 150 million years and is considered to be one of the oldest useful tools in existence. When you see depictions of dinosaurs, you always see the stegosaurus and family grazing together and always calm and disciplined. This is because the alpha-stegosaurus had mastered the use of "the tail" and all is under control. You will note that this is not so with the Tyrannosaurus or the Raptor for example. These creatures are all over the place, out of control, have a total lack of discipline and never eat their vegetables. Scientists are sure this had a lot to do with their extinction. The stegosaurus evolved into the chicken (see recipes in this book), but the others just vanished. Just think what a difference it would have made if the others used "the tail".

Made in the USA
Columbia, SC
14 January 2022

54213678R00142